YOUR PUBLIC SCHOOLS

What You Can Do to Help Them

by Barbara J. Hansen and
Philip English Mackey

CATBIRD PRESS

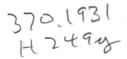

Catbird Press, 16 Windsor Road, North Haven, CT 06473
Catbird's books are distributed to the trade
by Independent Publishers Group.

Library of Congress Cataloging-in-Publication Data

Hansen, Barbara J.
Your public schools : what you can do to help them
by Barbara J. Hansen and Philip English Mackey
p.   cm.
Includes bibliographical references and index.
ISBN 0-945774-21-4 : $19.95
1. Home and school--United States. 2. Education--parent
participation--United States. 3 Public schools--United States.
4. Educational change--United States.
I. Mackey, Philip English. II. Title
LC225.3.H36   1993
370.19'31--dc20   93-24954 CIP

CONTENTS

What This Book Is About

This book is for people who care about our country's future and who know that its children *are* that future. It is for people who believe that public schools are an important element in the interlocking threads that hold our society together — public schools, not just schools in general, because only public schools offer *all* children an opportunity to acquire the skills and knowledge necessary to be productive citizens. This book is for people who understand that creating and maintaining good schools is a never-ending effort that requires the attention of everyone — not just educators, politicians, and parents of school-age children. If you're such a person, this book is for you.

How to Read This Book

This book is designed to be dipped into at any point. You don't need to read it from front to back (although that's fine, too). You can approach the contents from your own perspective, depending upon your particular interests and need for information.

The first part of the book contains a discussion of reasons why you need to get involved in public schools and some things you may want to consider before doing so. If what you're looking for are some specifics on ways to get involved, you might skip that part and go directly to the next section, which describes a number of strategies for you to consider. For those of you who want information on how public education evolved to its present state, what the public and researchers are saying about schools, a description of how schools operate, or suggestions on where you can find information about your schools, there is a third section that provides background information. If you are looking for assistance regarding something you are already doing or know that you want to accomplish, then the back of the book is where you might turn first.

This book has four major sections — Introduction, Strategies, Background Information, and Resources. The Introduction contains a discussion of some of the problems facing America's schools today and how your involvement can help to solve them. This section concludes with some major questions for you to consider before you decide how to direct your involvement.

Section Two contains specific strategies you can employ for getting involved in helping your public schools and then assisting in their improvement. You'll find help regarding some easy-to-do activities, such as voting and donating goods or services, as well as strategies that take more time and effort — and may have a bigger payoff. The strategies are organized by the amount of time and effort involved, from simple and occasional to full-time commitment. No matter how limited your time, you'll find something you can do to make the public schools better.

You will find that some suggestions and ideas are repeated from time to time. For instance, suggestions for how various skills can be applied to a school's benefit are included in more than one place. That is because this book is designed as a reference tool, one that will give you all the information you need wherever you first look. On occasion, however, you will be referred to another, related part of the book.

Section Three, Background Information, contains a capsule history of the public schools and how they arrived at their current state, as well as a look at efforts to reform the education system. Next is a brief review of what researchers say are the characteristics of effective schools and what the public thinks the schools should do. The section winds up with some advice on how you can increase your effectiveness in working with the public schools and where you can find information about them.

The last section is an annotated list of organizations that can provide you with additional information and advice — organizations as diverse as the National Committee for Citizens in Education, which is devoted to helping parents and other citizens be more effective in working with the schools; ASPIRA Association, Inc., a national Hispanic education leadership development organization; and the National Alliance of Business, which supports school-business partnerships. Addresses, telephone numbers and, where available, names of people to contact are included.

This section also includes a bibliography of books and articles you can read to increase your familiarity with public education issues, ideas about reforming public schools, and ways to become involved.

At the back of the book are several appendices, including a glossary of educational terms and additional information relating to school foundations and "I Have a Dream" projects.

Section One: INTRODUCTION

> "We don't have a child to waste. We will not be a strong
> country unless we invest in every one of our children . . .
> All children are essential to America's future."
> MARIAN WRIGHT EDELMAN[1]

Why *You* Need to Be Involved with Your Public Schools

Fundamentally, because there is no more important activity in the world than education. Of all charitable activities in which you might become involved, it is the most basic and the most important, because it has the capacity to solve many other problems in our society. Quality education can ameliorate poverty and urban decay; it can end bias. It can reduce the gap between rich and poor. It can provide new opportunities for racial/ethnic minorities, immigrants, the handicapped, women. It can shape the men and women of the 21st century, who will find ways to make our lives healthier and happier and to improve the way we affect our environment and the other species that share it with us. Education is the charitable activity from which all other hopes for human improvement spring.

But why be involved with public, rather than private or parochial schools? The answer is, because public schools are, or can be, the backbone of their communities. Good schools attract new residents to a community, and help keep its property values up. School athletic teams are a source of community pride. School events bring the community together, and provide it with entertainment. In some small towns, the public school is the focal point for community activities. That's where barbershop singers hold concerts, where local dance schools hold recitals, where everyone goes to vote, and where senior citizens groups meet.

Public schools are also important because they are the only schools where all children, regardless of their racial or ethnic background or their family's income, have a chance for an education.

And because the public schools are among the few places where children from varied backgrounds and social circumstances can learn how to get along with one another.

Are private and parochial schools better than public schools? Sometimes they are, but simply being private or parochial does not assure quality. And besides, private and parochial schools aren't open to everyone. Granted, some of them also have multi-ethnic and multi-racial student bodies, and there are some scholarships available for those who cannot afford tuition. But it takes knowledge and effort to get into these schools — knowledge that some parents don't have and effort they are unable to expend. How is a mother with minimal education supposed to make judgments about private or parochial schools? And how is she, overwhelmed with the demands of job and family, going to find the time — let alone the energy — to investigate alternative schools? Besides, even if she should settle on a particular private or parochial school, there is no guarantee that the school will accept her son or daughter. This is the real difference between private and public schools — not that one is better or worse than the other, but that private and parochial schools can choose their students while public schools accept all who arrive at their doors. America's public schools, for all their faults, are a symbol of what this country is supposed to be about — liberty and justice (through knowledge) for all.

As to why *you* should be involved, there are three good reasons: 1) the schools need help and you can be part of the solution; 2) it's your civic responsibility; and 3) good schools are in your self-interest.

The Schools Need Help and You Can Be Part of the Solution

America has rarely been satisfied with its schools. Every decade has had its share of school critics and education reformers. As we move into the 21st century, the debate is only going to get more vociferous. Even with all the recent efforts to improve education's "deteriorated house, ...the roof still leaks," says Harold Hodgkinson, director of the Center for Demographic Policy at the Institute for Educational Leadership. "There has been no change in high-school graduation rates, in most test scores, or in other indicators of 'quality.' "[2] In *What Do Our 17-Year-Olds Know?*, Diane Ravitch and Chester Finn declared, "If there were such a thing as a national report card for those studying American history and literature, then we would have to say that this nationally representative sample of 11th-graders earns failing marks on both subjects."[3]

A major criticism of America's schools has been aimed at student failures in science and math. U.S. students typically score well below students of similar age and grade level in the industrialized countries that are our economic competitors. In 1992, the Educational Testing Service's (ETS) *Second International Assessment of Educational Progress* reported that America's 9-year-olds finished a respectable 3rd among 10 participating nations in science, but 9th in mathematics. By age 13, American students had fallen further behind, finishing 14th of 15 nations in science and 13th of 15 in math.[4]

The cost of failing to teach the basics is high. U.S. businesses spend billions each year to train and retrain workers in the skills they should have learned in elementary school. In a job market increasingly requiring technological skills, about one in five adults lacks the basic skills and knowledge to function in society, and forty million are marginally illiterate.[5]

One of the reasons for such widespread illiteracy is the number of students who drop out of school before they graduate, although there has been some good news recently. According to the U.S. Education Department, the dropout rate for African-Americans aged 16-24 fell from 21.3 percent in 1972 to 13.6 percent in 1991, while the rate for non-Hispanic Caucasians fell from 12.3 percent to 8.9 percent. The bad news is that the rate for Hispanics went up from 34.3 to 35.3 percent during the same period.[6]

If you're like many Americans, you think these depressing statistics pertain to other people's schools. Sixty-four percent of parents and 40 percent of all respondents to the 1992 Gallup/Phi Delta Kappa poll gave grades of A or B to the public schools in their community. Only 18 percent, however, gave the same A or B to public schools nationally.[7]

Sometimes those As and Bs are accurate reflections of how well local schools are doing. But do you know for certain that your community's schools deserve such a high grade? How well do your students do on state-wide tests? What is the five-year trend of your district's college entrance examination scores? Do your schools ignore or mis-educate some students? What do you *really* know about your schools?

If your schools aren't doing so well, maybe it's because they are forced to struggle against tough odds. Gun-toting students are one of the horror stories we've been hearing about lately. Fortunately (for those not living in the worst of our inner cities, anyway), episodes of gunfire and other forms of violence are rare. But there are other, less obvious difficulties in some schools. For example, do you know how many different languages are spoken in your district's schools? Not how many are taught but, rather, how many children come to school unable to speak English? In a large district, students might speak more than a hundred different languages and dialects. Their parents may speak even less English, impeding their efforts to aid their children. Suburban areas may have it easier, but are not completely immune to this problem. It is not uncommon for a school in an ethnically mixed suburban community to have to deal with 15-20 different mother tongues. Having large numbers of foreign-born students may not be the most serious problem schools face, but it does require them to focus agreater proportion of their limited resources on bilingual and English-as-a-second-language programs than do other schools.

What kind of shape are your school buildings in? A poor physical environment can defeat the efforts of even the most innovative and competent teachers. Jonathan Kozol, in his book *Savage Inequalities*, describes one New York City classroom where a sixth grade of 30 children shares a room with 29 bilingual second graders. Each teacher has an assistant to help cope with the large class size. Thus, 63 people share a room that in a suburban school would probably house no more than 20 to 25 children and one teacher.[8] Also, many schools lack libraries and lab facilities — yours may be among them.

In 1983, several national organizations estimated that it would cost $25 billion to take care of the backlog of school repairs needed across the country, including such major items as plumbing, heating and cooling systems, electrical wiring, roofing, and asbestos removal. A 1988 study of urban districts showed that the problem had only gotten worse. Even newer buildings had substandard physical conditions, primarily because of "a serious lack of repairs and preventive maintenance."[9] By 1992, districts such as San Diego had cut their maintenance budgets to the bone. "Plugged toilets get fixed, but forget leaky roofs or broken drinking fountains," said one administrator.[10]

While urban districts and their problems get a lot of media (and government) attention, rural districts are engaged in a quieter struggle. Almost half of all school districts in the country are defined as rural (serving communities of fewer than 2,500 residents). A large percentage of their children come from families, most of them white, suffering from long-term poverty. Rural teachers tend to be less well-trained; almost a fifth of them report that they are unprepared or uncertified to teach at least one of their courses. More than half of the school buildings in these districts are rated substandard.[11]

Even if the schools in your community aren't in poor shape, there are probably needs going unmet. Many districts, for instance, are reducing or eliminating their music and art programs. "Art-on-a-cart," where part-time art teachers wheel their supplies around from classroom to classroom, has replaced separate art rooms in a number of elementary schools. Instrumental music instruction is also gone, along with bands and orchestras, and with them the opportunity for children to discover and develop their musical talents.

You Can Make a Difference

The public schools are part of the political process and, despite the pervading sense of impotence that many Americans feel about our political system, public education is one institution where individuals really matter. The next section of this book describes a multitude of ways you can make a difference, but here are a few examples of what others have done.

Gain a Computer Center/Save a School Library

Hakimah Abdulmalik, a nurse in New York City, joined with her fellow Parent-Teacher Association members in convincing a city councilwoman to give their school a grant for a computer lab. She was also part of a year-long project to reopen the school's library by helping uncrate and sort books that had been stored in the basement. "The only way it will work is for us to be involved," she says.[12]

Establish an Education Sunday Program

In southeast San Diego, California, Walter Kudumu was concerned about the lack of involvement of parents and other members of his disadvantaged community in the education of their children. So he got some school staff to join him in persuading local ministers to use their churches to help develop greater collaboration between the community and the education system. One Sunday each February — Education Sunday they call it — ministers emphasize the importance of education and share their pulpits with educators who talk about how parents and other community members can become involved in the schools. All adults, whether they are parents of school-age children or not, are urged to sign pledges promising "to encourage learning and success of children in school." Ministers follow up by recognizing successful students and by hosting special meetings where parents and others can learn how to access such services as tutoring, counseling, health screening, and information on college admissions and financial aid. Several hundred parents and other adults now participate in the program.[13]

Create a Support System to Help Kids Succeed

An anonymous donor in Hilton Head, South Carolina, has been instrumental in providing hope to a group of students in danger of not reaching their potential. His gift created a program, called STRIVE, that provides after-school tutoring, counseling, career advice, academic resources, and cultural opportunities for high-school students who might have been lost without it. What's more, his generosity sparked dozens of community members to volunteer as tutors and mentors and to get involved in the school.[14]

Encourage Good Citizenship Through Service to Others

Working out of her home in a small Vermont community, retired teacher Cynthia Parsons runs SerVermont, a program she created to instill a sense of service in young people. Her goals are to provide "better schooling for Vermont's children: more exploratory activities, more experiential opportunities, learning by doing translated into serving to learn and learning to serve." She also wants "to waken the public schools to their responsibility to produce 'small-d' democrats, . . . students prepared to be responsible citizens in a participatory democracy." Through her program, students integrate their schoolwork with the life of the community and learn what it means to be a good citizen.

Using small grants she solicits from foundations (she seeks no public funds), Parsons provides seed money to help students launch community service projects that help students learn at the same time they benefit their communities. Projects might involve gathering an oral history of the town, monitoring the water quality of a nearby river, or typing letters for arthritic senior citizens. But dispensing money is only a small part of Parsons' activity. She spends most of her time encouraging schools to set up service programs, providing suggestions for projects, and generally serving as a catalyst. Through her efforts, for instance, the Retired Senior Volunteer Program offered to provide all public schools with adult volunteers to act as liaisons between students wanting to volunteer and local agencies looking for help.

When Parsons began her program, only 10 of Vermont's high schools had any kind of community service activities. By the close of the 1991 school year, four years later, all but a handful had expanding programs, and every high school was conducting at least one project a year.[15]

Good Schools Are Your Responsibility

As corny as it sounds, it is your civic responsibility to be involved in the public schools. Lay control is an underlying principle of public education; that is why school boards are elected and why school governance is carried out at the local level. To quote Frank Kepple, former U.S. Commissioner of Education, "Schooling is too important to be left just to educators."

All citizens have an opportunity to get involved in public education, though few take advantage of it. Perhaps that's because most people rarely come in contact with the schools. Some 75% of today's U.S. adult population do not have school-age children. But even parents who have children in the public schools are often indifferent. Apathy is a national ailment.

How many times have you heard someone who rarely votes in school elections complain about the quality of local schools? Unfortunately, it happens all too often. When the community as a whole is not sufficiently committed to its schools or aware of its responsibility to them, schools fail. Children cannot be allowed to go undereducated. That is part of the social contract we have made as a nation. We were promised an education and our parents' generation saw to it that we got it. Now it is our turn to fulfill our obligation to future generations.

Good Schools Are in Your Self-Interest

You ignore public education at your own peril. Good schools benefit you, whether or not you have children or grandchildren attending them. Our country's future depends upon an educated workforce and a knowledgeable electorate.

America cannot keep its current standard of living, and certainly cannot grow, without millions of well-educated young people entering the workforce each year. Without the ability to handle rapidly-changing technology, young people are stuck in low-paying service jobs that do little to help the economy. Or worse, they end up unemployed, on welfare, selling drugs, or committing crimes. The monetary and social costs of undereducation are tragically high: the billions spent on the war on drugs, on the criminal justice system, and on prisons; the money wasted when poor people defer health care until they are forced to visit hospital emergency rooms; the debilitating social costs of welfare, homelessness, and hopelessness. It goes without saying that we all pay for these costs in dollars and in the pain that accompanies an economy and a society in decline. It is far more economical in the long run to ensure that everyone has the level of education necessary to get and hold the best job he or she is capable of.

Have you thought about what's going to happen when you retire? Are you, like so many others, counting on the income Social Security will provide? You do know, don't you, that Social Security is a pay-as-you-go system and not an insurance policy. Those of us currently in the workforce are supporting those who have already retired. And, contrary to popular myth, there is no surplus being built in Social Security funds. The Federal government is spending the "extra" money raised by the most recent Social Security tax increase as fast as it comes in.

So, who will be putting money into the system when *you* are taking it out? We won't be able to expect much if the workforce is primarily made up of undereducated people holding low-paying jobs. Our personal security is dependent on creating an educated workforce. And doing so means paying attention to the effectiveness of all our schools, regardless of where they are located. By the year 2000, the majority of schoolchildren will be from minority backgrounds. The adults they become will support our Social Security benefits — if we've educated them to hold good jobs.

The consequences of poor education are not just economic, however. If we fail to teach our neighbors' kids or the kids in the community down the road or in any of this country's towns and cities, we weaken the bonds that hold our society together. We are already witnessing some of these results in the alienation of ghetto youth and the failure of large numbers of Americans to vote in most elections.

As the country's demographics change, we will have to redefine who is "minority." Right now the political life of the nation is controlled primarily by white, middle- and upper-class males. But who will be making political decisions twenty or thirty years from now? To a large degree, it will be the children in our schools today. And in most major cities, that means children from African-American, Hispanic, or Asian-American families. If we expect these kids to be able to run our country tomorrow — or to vote intelligently for those who do — we'd better see to it that they have the know-how to do it well.

On a local level, property owners have a direct stake in public education: good schools boost property values. Realtors report that one of the most frequent questions house-seekers ask is, "How are the schools?" Increasing demand for housing in your community means money in your pocket when you sell your property. Businesses, too, are sure to consider the quality of public schools when deciding where to relocate or expand. If they choose your com- munity, they will benefit the local economy and your property taxes. On the other hand, if poor schools contribute to driving businesses out of your community, you will pay a price.

So, long-term or short-term, local or national, improving schools is one of the very best investments you can make.

Some Things to Consider

Before you take any action to help public schools, you might want to consider where your help is most needed, the skills and knowledge you have to offer, what your interests are, and the time you have available. In other words, you need a plan.

Which Community?

Your local schools may be what you think of first when you decide to put some time and energy into the public schools. Chances are they need your help and will be grateful for it. But they are not the only schools you could consider. According to a recent study by the National Research Council, more than a million people perform volunteer work in schools each year, but small schools, rural schools, and those with high minority enrollments attract relatively few of them. Almost half of schools with minority enrollments of 50 percent or more reported having no volunteers. Schools that need the most help are generally the ones least likely to have an interested or skilled community. All too often, students in these schools are unparented and caught in a poverty/welfare cycle. These are the kids who are struggling with the temptation to abuse drugs and alcohol, and who are in danger of violence at home and in the streets. Even where parents are present and caring, they often have little of the "free time" necessary for involvement. So think about investing your time in a district that really needs your help, whether it is your home community or not.

Elementary or Secondary?

If your interest is in working directly with children or with a single school in a multi-school district, you should give some thought to the age-level of the children you want to help. If, on the other hand, your assistance will be more remote (donation of office equipment and furniture, campaigning for top-quality school board members, work on behalf of a local education foundation, or participation in a school-business partnership), the age of the students may not make much difference to you.

If you are undecided about where to focus your energies, consider what it is you would like to achieve and where your talents lie. If you are comfortable with young children and interested in shaping young minds, then seek out a pre-school program or an elementary school and offer your assistance. Chances are you'll be welcomed with open arms, some of them tiny. Your contribution may be as simple as donating art supplies or reading stories to first graders. It may be as complex as recommending how the school should use its computers or serving on a school-site council.

If you are more interested in older children, you will also find plenty of opportunities. Adolescence is a particularly difficult period of life — all that yearning for acceptance as an adult, while lacking the maturity to handle the responsibilities, often results in self-destructive behavior. Adolescents need mentors and positive role models. The streets beckon with false promises of being "grown up," and someone needs to be there demonstrating that education and responsibility are also marks of an adult.

Of course, there are many other roles you can play in junior high or high schools. Older students are more likely to profit from infor-mation about your profession, your hobbies, your travels, your knowledge of a foreign language, your recollection of historic events. You may be able to provide employment or internships in your business for high-school students. You might speak at a career day program, join a booster club, or coach a team. You might lend your expertise in lighting, sound systems, art, sewing, accounting, or marketing to a student production of *Camelot*. No matter what you choose, you'll make a difference.

Your choice may be influenced by your own family situation. You might choose to work with, or on behalf of, students the same age as your own children or — if your children are now adults — as they were when you enjoyed them the most. If you are questioning whether to have children, you might like to spend time with the youngest students as a test of your readiness for the big move.

Local, State, or National?

Do you want to focus your energies on a single school, on a group of schools (such as a school district), or on state-wide action? Or is yours a national perspective? Access is a factor here. If your local school or district is closed off to you for some reason, you may want to concentrate on district-level political action (to get new blood on the school board, for instance) or work to establish — or dismantle — state laws and regulations.

The advantage of working in or with a single school is that you get to see the impact you can make as an individual. For example, the smile of a child or a word of gratitude from a teacher can tell you that you've done something to make their world better. When you operate at the district level — by serving on a board of education, for instance — the rewards may not be so direct. But this may be the place for you if you prefer working with adults. Also, consider that the impact of your success at district, state, and national levels is more far-ranging and can bring you public recognition as well as private pride.

Time Available

How much time do you have available — a few hours a week, a day or two a month, one day a year? Can you commit yourself to long-term activities that last for months or years, or is your schedule such that you can spare only brief periods of time? Do you have free time during the day, the evening, weekends, summer vacations? Your answers to these questions will help you focus on what you are *able* to do, which may be less than you *want* to do.

Some activities, such as serving as a tutor or mentor, require being available on a regular and frequent basis for at least one school year. The students you work with will depend on you to be with them for at least that long. Being an effective board of education member is also very time-consuming — far more than the one or two meetings a month that it looks like from the sidelines. And the commitment is for years, not months.

If you don't have that kind of time, yet want to make an impact on the district as a whole, you could volunteer to serve on an ad hoc board of education committee with a finite task, such as selecting a new superintendent. Other, less time-consuming activities include speaking to classes or demonstrating a skill; arranging for a field trip to your place of business; and helping organize one-time or annual school events, such as science or book fairs.

You can even become involved without sacrificing much time at all. Some of the strategy suggestions in the following section, such as contributing supplies and equipment, require little time and no long-term commitment.

Skills and Interests

This is the heart of the matter. What do you enjoy doing and what are you good at? Do you enjoy being with children? Then serving as a classroom volunteer, a coach, a mentor, or a tutor is likely to attract you. Do you prefer the company of adults? Joining a group advocating school improvement or helping set up an education foundation for your district may be activities you would enjoy. Are you good at keeping things organized? Those skills can be put to good use in classrooms, school offices, and libraries — and would be most welcome in an election campaign. Whatever you choose to do, make sure it is something that will make you happy, something that gives you a chance to do what you enjoy. Here are some other ideas:

Skills & Interests	Activities
Children's Health and Safety	Join or help form advisory committees to help schools improve lunch, health, counseling, or anti-drug programs; join fellow citizens in crime-watch programs near the schools or in your neighborhood.
Computers	Help set up school computer systems; tutor students and/or teachers; donate or solicit donations of equipment and software.
Construction	Help rebuild a playground; advise shop classes; assist students in building science fair displays; donate building materials.

Travel	Present programs on different cultures in places you've visited.
Photography	Teach a mini-course on composition or photographic techniques; seek donations for a darkroom and help set it up; advise student newspaper or yearbook photographers.
Sports	Coach a team; join a booster group; work with individual youngsters who need help in developing their skills.
Politics	Assist in election campaigns and budget referenda; serve on a school board; lobby for your cause.
Public relations	Help the school or district set up a PR program; help generate interest in school affairs; volunteer your skills to an advocacy group.
Teaching	Tutor; mentor; serve as classroom aide; present special programs to students; become a teacher.
Reading	Tutor; serve as a library aide; be a storyteller; serve on a curriculum advisory committee.
Organizing others	Start a volunteer program; set up a school-business partnership or an education foundation; run a school board campaign.
Persuading others	Become a citizen advocate; serve on a school council; join a school board; lobby for legislative or regulatory changes.

Clearly, these are but a few of the things you can do. See the Strategies section for more ideas.

A Caution

Some schools and school districts welcome parents and other members of the community and will respond with alacrity to your offer of help. Boards of education in these districts scrupulously operate in the "sunshine" and invite public input into their decisions. They go above and beyond any state requirements about providing information on the district and how well it is doing. Principals and teachers in these districts welcome visitors to their schools and encourage volunteers to work with them.

Others, unfortunately, operate like fortresses. Staff in these schools and districts see parents and other community members as nuisances and — in extreme cases — threats. "We know what's best for children," is their attitude, "and we don't need anyone to tell us what we should be doing." Boards in these districts evade (if not violate) open meeting laws and rarely respond to public questioning and criticism. They may frequently go into closed or "executive" sessions, or conduct board business by telephone. School personnel may make parents and others uncomfortable about visiting their buildings by requiring appointments well in advance or by displaying signs such as this actual example:

> Warning! City Ordinance 54:32 requires that all visitors to a public school shall report immediately upon entering to the office of the principal and shall state their reasons for entry and business to be transacted. Violators are subject to a $500 fine or six months in jail or both. Welcome to your school.

Most districts and schools lie somewhere in between these two extremes. Their board members and staff are well-intentioned, if not always responsive. Public input is welcomed, but often not actively sought or effectively used. Schools are open to parents and have effective volunteer programs, but some staff, administrators, and board members may be reluctant to involve "outsiders" in their deliberations or activities.

This reluctance can stem from several sources. Some board members and staff may feel intimidated by the presence of parents and other citizens due to personal insecurities, bad previous experiences, or a lack of training in how to work with them effectively. They are concerned about being judged, analyzed, and talked about. Others may be hide-bound, caught in the status quo, and threatened by new ideas. Still others may accept offered help, but expect volunteers to do as they are told, without asking questions.

So, as you begin to interact with school personnel, go slowly. Remember to ask rather than tell, and try to build trust. At the same time, watch out for people who may sabotage your efforts, either maliciously or unwittingly, and attempt to build strong contacts with those who are supportive of what you are trying to do.

Section Two: STRATEGIES

Your opportunities to aid schools and school districts range from very simple to complex, time-consuming activities. Our list is not exhaustive, nor are the items mutually exclusive. Some school districts offer other opportunities, and you may choose to create your own. The idea here is to stimulate your thinking about ways you can help improve your public schools.

Vote

A simple, but largely unrecognized way for you to aid public education is to vote.

Each state handles governance of education differently. Some hold direct elections of school board members, either in special school elections or at primary and general elections. Others authorize elected government officials to appoint school officials. Some states combine both methods. School budgets and the issuance of bonds for major construction projects are voted on directly in some places, but not others. If you live in one of the states where school board members or school levies are voted upon in special elections, your vote may carry an inordinate amount of weight. In some places, the percentage of registered voters who turn out for such elections is minuscule — as low as five percent. One vote can turn back a referendum or elect a board member.

Voting for School Board Candidates

Voting intelligently, however, requires being informed about candidates, issues, and proposals. Before casting your ballot for board candidates, for instance, you'll want to know something about how they will approach their responsibilities and to what extent their opinions are compatible with yours:

- What are their priorities (special education, math and science, computers, better athletic facilities, more pay for teachers)?

- What opinions do they hold about specific education policies that are important to you?

- Are they single-issue candidates, fixated on firing the superintendent of schools or eliminating such "frills" as art and music?

- What is their philosophy of education (teacher-centered or child-centered instruction; the role of tests and grades; the relative importance of teaching facts, developing reasoning skills, and affecting behavior)?

- If a budget proposal is also on the ballot, do they support it? Why or why not?

- What experience have they had that might lead them to be good board members?

- Are they prepared for the long hours and frustrating state restrictions that many board members complain about (at the very least, you don't want to vote for candidates who will quit halfway through their first term)?

- Are they aligned with a particular political faction or party? What kind of influence might this have on them?

- What long-term political ambitions do they have? There's nothing wrong with looking ahead to further political office, but you'll want to make sure they are committed to serving well in this one.

As you gather information, you will soon discover that candidates' opinions, intentions, and character are far more important than their status. Is the candidate a parent of children in the school system or a senior citizen? A teacher in another district, a spouse of an employee in your district, or someone with no connection to school personnel? A lawyer, an accountant, or a housewife? An Hispanic or an Asian-American? None of it makes much difference in comparison with what candidates believe, what they say they want to accomplish, and their records of integrity and hard work.

One way to gain the information you need is to read your local newspapers. They will run articles about candidates and their stands on issues of immediate concern. Another is to attend "candidates nights," where you can hear those running for office speak about what is important to them, and where you can also ask them questions. If these forums are not offered in your community, they should be; encourage your church, PTA, or other community organization to sponsor one. A third possibility is to attend, or host, an informal gathering where one or more candidates can speak with members of the community. You can also talk to friends who take an interest in school affairs to see whom they are supporting and why. Similarly, you can watch for newspaper ads or flyers to see who is endorsing whom. When people you respect are supporting a particular candidate, you may be encouraged about the individual's qualifications and beliefs.

The recent phenomenon of "stealth" candidates makes it all the more important that you learn about your school board candidates and, if possible, get them to state their views in public. Stealth candidates are would-be board members with secret agendas arising from their religious or philosophical convictions. Some communities have already had the unpleasant experience of seeing seemingly bland candidates turn into disruptive ideologues once they are elected.

This is not to suggest, of course, that people with unorthodox or extremist views should be barred from running for school boards or that you shouldn't vote for them. You and your fellow citizens simply deserve to know just what they are voting for, and you may be able to help the process. If there are candidates you and your friends don't know much about, ask them to take a public stand on such litmus-test issues as banning books from the school library, teaching evolution, the proper content of sex education courses or, more generally, what impact their religious and philosophical views are likely to have on their actions as board members. Stealth candidates may respond to such questions by hiding their true beliefs, of course, but they may find it harder to act on them in the face of the public statements you have elicited.

Becoming informed about school board candidates takes time, but it's time well spent. You can't hire educators or determine what is taught in your schools, but you can decide who will make those decisions, and you can make sure they are the most qualified people to do so.

Voting for Budget and Bond Issues

When the question on the ballot is whether to support or reject a budget or bond issue, you can make yourself more knowledgeable by reading information the school district provides, attending informational meetings (such as budget hearings), reading newspaper articles and letters to the editor, talking with knowledgeable friends and neighbors, and personally reviewing the budget (for more about budgets, see pages 171-174) or bond-issue documents (they are available to the public at the school district office and, perhaps, at libraries and other locations).

Here are some questions you might want to find answers to before voting on a school budget:

- What percentage increase or decrease is this proposal relative to the current budget? Is the change due to enrollment increases, school improvement programs, inflation?

- Where will additional monies be spent? Where will cuts be made? Are they in areas you feel are appropriate?

If the vote is on the issuance of bonds for capital improvements, especially the purchase, construction, or repair of buildings, you might want to ask:

- Why is this necessary? Has the school population grown? Are buildings unsafe? Have new state regulations mandated changes? Does the use of modern technology require upgraded buildings?

- What other methods for solving the problem were explored and why were they rejected?

- If the money is to be spent on a new school building, what provisions are being made in its design to permit easy transformation to other uses if the school population should drop?

Whether the proposal is about a budget or a capital improvement, you will want to know the bottom line: how will it affect your taxes? A bond issue means incurring long-term debt, and the repayment usually means a tax increase. Often, school districts will publish information about the amount of additional tax dollars the bond will require each year for property valued at $50,000, $100,000, $200,000, and so forth. If your district doesn't furnish this information on its own (look in newspapers and ask at the local library), call the superintendent's office and ask for it. If the district can't or won't supply the information, they certainly don't care much about securing your vote.

Annual budgets usually, but not always, require an increase in taxes, if only to cover the costs of inflation. Districts can sometimes cover increased costs without more taxes by using unappropriated surplus funds that have accumulated over several years, or because the municipality has acquired new ratables (i.e., taxable properties). Occasionally, a decreasing budget may actually lower your tax burden.

It is, of course, short-sighted to automatically vote "no" on your school budget because it will increase your taxes, just as it is to vote "yes" solely because it won't. It is important to you, your fellow taxpayers, and students in your community that your vote helps to ensure that money is wisely spent.

Voting for Other Officials

School elections aren't the only forum, however, where your vote can influence education. Municipal, state, and federal officials all influence education policy and finance. One of the issues in the 1992 presidential election, for instance, was who would be the true "education president." Remember, too, that members of Congress vote each year on the amounts of money to be spent from the national treasury on education and education-related programs (such as Head Start). They also help shape education policy through legislation, such as laws forbidding discrimination.

State governors have been leading the charge for education reform in recent years. President Clinton, who was instrumental in instituting a number of significant changes when he was governor of Arkansas, is just one example. Governors and state legislators across the country have addressed such issues as improved teacher preparation; competency testing for students, teachers and administrators; teacher salaries; and distribution of funds among school districts. Some have encouraged innovative approaches. Kentucky abolished its state education department, for instance, and created a new system for governing schools. Minnesota's legislature created "charter schools" — a program where teachers can create their own schools and have them funded at the state's average per pupil expenditure. Charter school teachers can choose to be employees of non-profit corporations with collective bargaining rights, or to own their schools through professional partnerships.

Municipal officials often have a great deal to say about their communities' school districts, even when they do not have any real authority. When their informal influence fails to bring about changes they seek, mayors and council members have been known to take their quarrels with public school officials to the electorate as a means of applying pressure. Of course, in those towns where the mayor appoints school board members and controls the school district budget, their influence is even more keenly felt.

So voting is not a "little thing" when it comes to education. Your vote counts and, in some elections, will be very influential on the direction of your school district. It takes a little effort to vote wisely, but it is time well spent.

Donate Money and Goods

If you're like most Americans, you give donations to worthwhile organizations each year: money to some; goods, like used books, clothing, and furniture, to others. You may help support your church or synagogue, medical research organizations, social service agencies, and animal shelters. What about supporting quality education in your community or in less fortunate communities in your vicinity? You'd be surprised how important your donation could be to teachers, who sometimes have to struggle to do their jobs with meager resources.

When you give something to a school district, or to any other non-profit organization, you can make it an unrestricted or a restricted gift. If it is unrestricted, district administrators can do whatever they like with it. They may decide to put your computer in school A or school B, in a classroom or in the business manager's office — or in a closet, for that matter. They will place your unrestricted cash donation in a general fund, where it may be used for any purpose: maybe for exciting new lab equipment, maybe for fuel oil.

Unrestricted gifts are easiest for a school district to deal with (so easy that, for most districts, no gift is too small) and are no doubt what administrators prefer. But you may get more satisfaction from restricting your gift to a particular school or a particular purpose. You have every right to set restrictions on how your donation is used, but of course the district has every right to turn down the gift if your restrictions are objectionable. Thus, a district would almost certainly accept a donation for purchase of library books, but might reject restrictions stipulating the exact books to buy or requiring that the books be placed in a school that already has the best library in the district. You are also likely to meet with rejection if the amount of your gift is less than the administrative costs of adhering to your restrictions. Other reasonable restrictions are that your money be spent on science lab equipment, landscaping, girls' sports, hall decorations, computers, teacher amenities (new desks, improvements to the staff lounge), the sixth grade, class trips, prizes for top students, or the music program.

To give a restricted gift, call the school district office and tell the business administrator what you have in mind. If he or she indicates that your restrictions are acceptable, make a note on the check about the intended use and send it in. If the school district has a problem with your restrictions, they will probably suggest a related use, especially if the donation you have in mind is a significant sum.

You can't afford to give your schools a cash donation? What about giving them some of those things you've been storing in the attic or garage? "One man's trash is another man's treasure," the saying goes, and you'd be surprised at the variety of used goods a school might want. There is probably a school near you that would welcome:

Aquariums or terrariums
Board games, such as chess, checkers, or Scrabble
Books or magazine subscriptions for the library or for
    classrooms
Carpeting
Collections of stamps, coins, butterflies, seashells
Computer hardware or software
Desks, chairs, bookcases, and filing cabinets for teachers
    or administrators
Hand-held calculators
Houseplants
Musical instruments
Office supplies
Old clothes (for skits, pageants, plays)
Pots and pans for home economics classes
Prints of famous paintings for art classes or to brighten
    the halls and cafeteria
Records, tapes, and compact disks
Refrigerators
Room air conditioners
Rugs
Sports equipment
Television sets
Tools or supplies for the maintenance staff
Toys for elementary-school students
Videos about animals, famous people, foreign countries,
    historical events

Beyond such small items, you might consider giving more substantial property. Some schools will accept donations of old cars, to use in vocational training classes. It's also possible that the school district would be eager to get a piece of land to use as an environ-mental center, a playground, or a site for future construction.

Whether you're giving money or goods to the schools, you'll have to clear it with the school or district office. In some cases, it may be more convenient for you or for the school district if you make a gift by way of a third party, such as a parents organization, a scholarship fund, or a local education foundation. The district office can tell you how to reach such groups.

Regardless of what you give or how you give it, remember that it may earn you a tax deduction. If you intend to claim a deduction for a gift of goods, be sure to establish their fair market value by determining what similar goods, in similar condition, are selling for. For gifts of over $5,000 in value, you will need to provide the IRS with an appraisal.

Serve As a School Volunteer

Personally working in schools and, if it is your bent, with students is a direct way of helping improve the quality of education in your district. Schools can always use another hand, and some desperately need as many as they can get. Whatever you can offer, no matter how little, is more than what could be done without you. Because volunteering allows you to see the direct results of your efforts, it can be the most rewarding of all the activities mentioned in this book. And it can actually benefit your health. Two Cornell University sociologists have found that people engaged in volunteer work tend to live longer and are less likely to suffer major illnesses. So by volunteering in the public schools, you'll not only make this country a better place to live in, you may even live in it longer![16]

Activities

What might you do? The list is almost endless. In alphabetical order, here are a few ideas:

- **Arts Instructor:** If you have a skill or talent, such as music, painting, sculpture, dance, drama, or crafts, you may be welcomed to work with groups of children in your area of interest. You can discuss your own work, demonstrate techniques, give tours of studios or galleries, or give slide shows on your favorite artist or topic. In many schools, music and art programs are the first to be cut in hard times, so there may be a great need for your skills and ideas.

- **Career Consultant:** Career education is an important part of schooling. You can inform students about career opportunities in your field, the prerequisites for being hired, what you like and dislike about your profession, and what kind of lifestyle your career can offer. A chemist can provide fascinating, "real-world" information for chemistry students, an editor for English students, and so forth. At the high-school level, you might also give students tips on preparing resumes and interviewing for entry-level jobs.

- **Classroom Aide**: You can be a part-time or full-time classroom aide and assist teachers by preparing and organizing class materials, checking tests, keeping records, collecting papers, distributing materials, giving make-up tests, and working with students in special projects. Or you can serve as an aide in the school library, guidance office, lunchroom, or playing field. See p. 126 for more information.

- **Club Sponsor:** You can sponsor or help with a special interest club, such as making videos, puppetry, needlework, computers, stamp or coin collecting, chess, poetry, doll making, carpentry, gardening, rocks and minerals, photography, or dance. Many schools offer clubs like these and are also on the lookout for sponsors with different interests so that new ones can be created.

- **Coach:** You're good at football, swimming, tennis, golf, ping pong, basketball, chess, or badminton. Or maybe you're not all that good, but you've been playing for a long time and you could sure give students some valuable pointers. Whatever your skill level, there is probably a school that would welcome you as an assistant coach or maybe as a referee or umpire. You'll be of great help to the staff member in charge of the activity and to the kids. And you'll have a great time being involved with a sport you love.

- **Collector:** Do you have a special collection of some sort — stamps, postcards, seashells, model planes, butterflies? Your local school would probably love to set up a special display and have you come in to talk about it.

- **Compassionate Ear:** School health clinics are becoming more common, especially in high schools. Many welcome volunteers who will listen with compassion to confused, frightened, and lonely young people who are dealing with pregnancy, drug or alcohol problems, and family violence.

- **Computer Consultant:** Computers are being used more and more in schools. But not many teachers are proficient in their use. If you are, you can provide computer instruction for students or teachers, help the school decide what hardware and software to buy, or help set up systems.

- **Decorator:** The physical appearance of a school should evoke harmony, liveliness, excitement, and joy. But too many are poorly designed and drably decorated. If you have professional or amateur skills as a decorator, gardener, or landscaper, you may be able to help change the whole atmosphere of the building. You will have to work closely with the teachers, of course, and provide plenty of opportunities to display student art and decoration. You may be able to enlist local artists or gallery owners to help you lead a community effort to improve the looks of classrooms, hallways, playgrounds, the auditorium, the teachers lounge, and the cafeteria. If you do, you may have a profound effect on the children and adults who spend so much of their lives in and around the building.

- **Drug Counselor:** Drug use is a national scandal. Many schools and school districts are looking for ways to keep their students from becoming part of the problem. You can help by assisting school personnel to set up and run a drug and alcohol awareness program.

- **Field Trip Host:** Is your workplace one that might interest young people? Fire houses, police stations, and airports are obvious field trip possibilities, but so are greenhouses, farms, manufacturing firms, and banks, to name just a few. You can offer to host or conduct a visit.

- **Health Instructor:** If you are a nurse, doctor, paramedic, or other health professional, you can teach cardio-pulmonary resuscitation (CPR) to health classes. Or you can give talks on sex education, nutrition, and other health-related topics.

- **History Instructor:** You can be a living history lesson. What was it like to live through the Depression or the Holocaust, to participate in civil rights marches or anti-war demonstrations, to fight in Vietnam, to visit a divided Berlin, to watch the Watergate investigation unfolding, to live through a major event in your town's history? Offer to give a talk in or outside a class, or allow yourself to be interviewed by students (that way you're sure to stay on their level).

- **Internship Sponsor:** You can offer student or teacher internships at your workplace in the summer, after school, or on weekends. They can be as short as a week or two, or last for an entire school year. There's nothing like seeing how things work in the real world to enrich a teacher's lessons or stimulate a high-school student's imagination and initiative. Teacher internships might take the form of "shadowing," in which the teacher accompanies a research chemist, a financial analyst, a store manager, or a mason, as the employee carries out his or her normal duties. Student internships might also involve shadowing, but are more likely to be more "ordinary" jobs, which reinforce classroom lessons or teach general workplace skills. Student internships might involve the best students in a school — rewarding excellent classroom performance with desirable work opportunities — or they might offer poor students a chance for acquiring skills and developing self-reliance that would be hard to achieve in the conventional part-time job market. Or you can hire a student (see p. 47).

- **Language Instructor:** If you are fluent in another language, you can provide bilingual assistance to children who are not proficient in English, or give extra conversational practice to students in foreign-language classes. Even if English is your only language, you can help non-English speaking students practice newly learned vocabulary.

- **Lecturer:** You can offer to speak to classes on subjects that interest you. If horticulture is your vocation or avocation, for instance, you might demonstrate seed germination to kindergarteners or how to determine soil acidity to older students. A city planner might discuss urban renewal or current zoning problems with high-school students. On a more general level, you could talk to classes about current issues, such as energy conservation, crime and punishment, modern architecture, or inflation.

- **Library Assistant:** If libraries are your interest, you can catalog books, type, read or tell stories, listen to children read stories, tape their stories, help them with audio-visual equipment, research a particular topic for a teacher, or help students conduct research and select books.

- **Performer:** Can you juggle? Perform magic tricks? Play the piano? Volunteer to share your talent with students, either for a general assembly or for a single class. Of course, your performance will be more welcome if you can tie it to some educational activity — the physics of juggling, for instance, or the cultural origins of different piano styles and pieces. Like many volunteer activities, this one can be of great value to the volunteer, providing exposure to eager audiences.

- **Publication Advisor:** If you've always enjoyed writing, you might coordinate a writing project and help produce a booklet of student stories and poetry. Or you can provide advice to students working on a school newspaper, literary magazine, or yearbook. Skills and knowledge in editing, photography, graphic design, typesetting, desktop publishing, and printing would be helpful here.

- **Reader:** Like to read aloud? You can tape-record textbooks so that students with reading problems can listen to a cassette as they read their assignments. Or tape poetry, short stories, or plays for students to listen to at school or at home.

- **Science Project Consultant:** Are you interested in science and concerned about kids who don't have parents with the time or ability to help them undertake science projects? You can volunteer to help one of them or, even better, organize a pool of volunteers to assist any child that wants help.

- **Theatrical Director:** At the middle and high school levels, finding someone to direct student theatrical productions is often a difficult proposition. While it's rarely an easy task, your reward for taking on the assignment will be a bunch of excited and grateful kids. Or you can offer to help with lighting, sound, costumes, scenery design and construction, or prompting.

- **Transport Provider:** There are probably other people in your community, especially senior citizens, who would be glad to help out in the schools if they only had some way to get there. You can provide transportation for them.

- **Travel Speaker:** Like to travel? You might show slides or videos from the places you have visited, especially foreign countries, and talk about customs of other cultures.

- **Tutor:** You can tutor youngsters, working one-on-one or with small groups, perhaps concentrating on specific learning problems in reading or math.

- **Video Enthusiast:** Help build the school's library of educational videotapes by seeking donations of surplus tapes from video stores, duplicating tapes in the public domain, or seeking funds to buy new tapes. Or offer to tape children's skits, guest speakers, or classroom lessons — such as physics demonstrations — that are difficult to duplicate.

- **Writer:** Let's face it. A lot of people who need to write well just don't have the knack. If you do, you might volunteer to coach student writers, lead a student writers group, teach writing skills to after-school or Saturday classes, or even hold a writing seminar for teachers.

Not all school volunteers work with students. Some give their time to teachers or administrators. If you're a scientist, for instance, you can offer to teach teachers the latest findings in your field. A historian can offer to consult on the purchase of new history texts. An outplacement counselor might advise career education staff on changes in the job market. A business executive can provide advice on financial or administrative practices. A writer might volunteer to develop a grant proposal. Whatever your skill or talent, the schools can use it.

How to Get Started

If you decide to get involved at a particular school, call the school office and make your offer. If the school has a volunteer program, you'll be directed to the person in charge. If not, you may be referred to one of the school's administrators or to a teacher who has mentioned wanting the sort of help you are offering. If the school seems uninterested, or does not return your call for some reason, phone the district office or the parent organization to see if they are any more receptive.

If there is a teacher, librarian, or other staff member you particularly want to work with, you might approach him or her directly, but if you do, be sure the principal or the school's volunteer coordinator is informed of what the two of you are planning, so that your activities can be integrated with other volunteer efforts in the school, and so school staff will know who you are when they see you in the building. Student safety requires careful monitoring of people coming into the school.

If you prefer to get involved at the district level or have no preference as to which school you work in, call the district superintendent's office and ask to speak with the district's volunteer coordinator (if there is such a position). He or she should be able to tell you the range of volunteer opportunities in the school district and direct you to the person you need to speak with. If the district doesn't have a coordinator, ask to speak with the administrator in chargeof instruction. In smaller districts, this may be the superintendent of schools. These people, like school-level staff, are usually very approachable, especially when they know you are offering your help. Most will go out of their way to assist you.

In some communities, another avenue for volunteering is through programs sponsored by local organizations, such as a local volunteer center or clearinghouse, PTAs, or the Retired Senior Volunteer Program (RSVP).

Before you leap into a volunteer position, however, there are some things you might want to ascertain. Talk to other volunteers (if you don't know any, ask the volunteer coordinator to give you some names) and with school staff and administrators to get answers to these questions.

- How serious is the school staff about wanting volunteers, and what are their expectations? Some schools may want volunteers only for routine work. If you're looking for an active role in making school a better place for kids, you might be better off in a school that wants people to be directly involved with students.

- What kind of orientation to the school will you be given? Be sure it's a solid one. Ask for any written guidelines and rules.

- Does everyone understand what it is you will be doing, and how and when it will be done? If you are going to be doing more than a one-shot activity, ask for a written job description or, if one isn't available, request a verbal one. Take notes, write up the description, and share it with the person who will be in charge of your work.

- What is the chain of command? Whom will you report to? Will that person conduct an evaluation of your efforts and provide you with feedback on them? What kind of support and supervision can you expect from others in the school?

- Where will you be working? Make sure you are given an orderly and clearly designated place to work and the equipment, supplies, and tools to do the expected job.

By the way, your expenses as a school volunteer are tax deductible, but your time is not.

Secrets of a Successful Volunteer

There is more to volunteering than showing up at the designated time and place. Here are some tips to make your efforts successful.

- **Make commitments you can keep.** Don't bite off more than you can chew. Start with a limited number of hours and increase them if you find you enjoy what you are doing and the need for your time is sufficient. Be aware that volunteering is not always convenient and that students and teachers will come to depend on you. If you take on a tutoring or mentoring responsibility, you cannot involve yourself in that child's life and then just disappear.

- **Be thorough and conscientious** in what you do and how you prepare for it. Whatever your task is, it is important in some way to the education of children. If you can't or aren't interested in doing it well, don't volunteer for it and don't allow yourself to be assigned to it.

- **Be punctual.** Classrooms operate by the clock. If a teacher is expecting you to assist students with developing their readingskills, for instance, showing up during the math period won't be much help.

- **Be pleasant, stay flexible, and maintain a positive attitude.** If problems occur, seek constructive solutions instead of griping. Be prepared for changes in routine and adapt to the unexpected. Have fun with what you are doing and share your pleasure in it with students and staff.

- **Maintain confidentiality** about individual students, and don't gossip about the school family.

- **Be patient and a good listener.** Allow trust to develop between you and the students and between you and the school staff.

- **Make sure you are doing something you enjoy and** will not become bored with quickly. And, just as important, be sure it is something you can **do well**. An incompetent volunteer may be worse than no volunteer and, in fact, may make students and school staff leery of all volunteers.

Get Other People Involved in Volunteering

If you're convinced that volunteering your services can help improve your schools, imagine what you could accomplish if you recruited 10 or 50 volunteers! Here's a step-by-step approach you can take to create a volunteer program in your school or school district:

Step 1 — The first things you'll need are (i) the support of school staff where the program will be implemented and (ii) community people interested in getting a volunteer program underway.

You will want to discuss your idea with principals and teachers to determine how they feel about such a program and to gain their help in starting the program and placing volunteers once it is under way. The best way to approach this task is to meet individually with principals to explain your intentions and to ask them to talk with their teachers.

When you have the support of one or more schools, you will be ready to talk with the board of education and the superintendent about your plans and to solicit their approval. The simplest way to approach them is to ask to be placed on the agenda of a board work session. Call the board secretary and tell him or her you'll need only a few minutes of the board's time. The superintendent attends these meetings also. Once there, present your idea for a volunteer program and the benefits it will offer the school or school district — just as you have done with the principals — and sketch out for them how you propose establishing the program. If possible, have one or more of the principals who are supporting your idea (or some teachers from their schools) talk about their interest in the program.

Meanwhile, bring together a group of community members interested in education and introduce them to the concept of a school volunteer program. One place to start is with parent-teacher groups in each targeted school. You can also ask the schools to publicize their interest in such a program in their communications with parents. Local congregations and community organizations are other places to look for potential co-organizers. Be patient, however. You may have to host several such meetings before you can develop a nucleus of people committed to helping you get the program started.

Once you have your group of organizers, form a coordinating

council consisting of them and of school staff (support staff as well as teachers) who are seriously interested in pursuing the idea. The council will then define the program's goals and objectives and decide how the program will operate.

Step 2 — Once again, approach the district superintendent and the school board for their input and approval — this time with a program plan, not just a concept. They will want to know:

How the program will operate;

How it will be administered, governed, and evaluated;

What it will cost;

The degree to which professional staff are committed to implementing it.

Step 3 — Each participating school will need to identify a volunteer coordinator. This might be a school staff member, but it could also be an interested community member.

Step 4 — Some start-up funding may be needed for such things as postage, paper, printing costs, and perhaps staff time. If the school district doesn't absorb these costs, many will have to be raised by the coordinating council. Local businesses can help here.

Step 5 — Recruit volunteers. You will want to get the active cooperation of businesses, unions, universities, government agencies, and the media to activate employees, retirees, and the public to volunteer.

Talk to community organizations and service clubs — Rotary, Kiwanis, Lions, Masons, veterans' groups, the League of Women Voters, the American Association of University Women, Chamber of Commerce, the Junior League, garden clubs, houses of worship and religious groups, and neighborhood associations. Seek out volunteers in housing developments, senior apartment complexes, senior citizen centers, and condominiums. Stress that school volunteers need not be, and often are not, parents of school-age children and that the skills and interests of volunteers will be used — that there are a lot more than clerical tasks available. Talk about the many different types of help needed.

Put posters, flyers, and bookmarks in libraries, adult centers, social services offices, shopping centers, and supermarkets. Send flyers home with children. Be sure you don't exclude any groups; if there is a large number of foreign speakers in your community, print flyers in their languages.

Seek all free opportunities for publicity — bus ads, bus bench signs, billboards, etc. Submit articles to local newspapers (don't forget the giveaway type), get PTAs to make announcements. Local radio and television stations will often broadcast brief public service announcements and might even help you write one. Contact your local United Way and volunteer organizations. Some of them publish or keep directories of volunteer openings. Ask the human resources departments of local corporations to publish articles about your program in their newsletters and to post flyers on their bulletin boards.

Make an effort to solicit volunteers from all the different racial, ethnic, and economic groups in your community. Recruit both men and women. Pay particular attention to your community's senior citizens — the most rapidly expanding age group in the country and an insufficiently tapped resource for the public schools. More than 25 percent of people over 55 already volunteer their time to charities and, according to a recent survey, more would be willing and able to do so if they were asked.[17] These are people with talents, skills, energy, time, accumulated knowledge, compassion, and years of experience in human relations. Yet compared with hospitals, museums, and many other organizations, schools get little of the benefit of their skills.

Step 6 — Volunteer training sessions will be needed in each participating school. At a minimum, they should include discussion of:

- The school's and the program's written guidelines and rules;

- A description of activities volunteers can choose to be involved with, and how and when each activity is to be done;

- Whom volunteers will be working for, plus the chain of command within the school and throughout the district;

- How they and the program will be evaluated;

- The supplies and support that will be provided to help them do the job.

Training does not have to be formal in any sense. The school volunteer coordinator might handle it with a telephone call and a brochure or letter.

Step 7 — Match volunteers with activities. You'll want to be sure volunteers are placed in situations that take advantage of their interests and abilities. The coordinating council may want to screen volunteers by having them fill out a skills and interests inventory or by interviewing them, with final selection left to the school principal or teachers.

Step 8 — Implement an evaluation system — one that is simple to administer, yet provides the kinds of information you need to make good decisions about individual volunteers and how they are used. Seek input from volunteers as well as from those they work with (including students). The information you gather should be used to weed out incompetent volunteers; find better placements for those whose skills are being under- or misused or are unhappy for other reasons; strengthen the screening process to avoid misplacements; identify the strengths and weaknesses of the program; and identify new ways that volunteers can be used. Plans for the next year will be based on the results of your evaluation.

Step 9 — Plan and conduct an appreciation event for volunteers (thank you letters, luncheon, etc.)

For more ideas about how to recruit and use volunteers, see the sections on organizing advocacy campaigns (pages 114-120), establishing local educational foundations (pages 93-101), and getting your company involved (pages 41-48). Also see the section on creating a skills directory (pages 78-82), which can be an important part of a volunteer organizing effort.

It takes a considerable amount of time to establish an effective school volunteer program, but it's worth it. Chances are that your schools will benefit enormously from the talent and energy your volunteers provide and from the increased community support such programs create.

Take Part in Your Company's Activities in Support of Schools

Your company may already be involved in improving American schools. If not, it should be — out of simple self-interest, if nothing else — and you may be able to play a role in encouraging the process.

The best way to find out if your company is already active is to contact its community affairs or public affairs office. If there are no educational improvement activities at your location, ask about other company facilities. What do you care about the Dallas office if you work in Michigan? Maybe the Michigan management can be persuaded to replicate a program that has proved itself elsewhere.

If your company has existing programs to help schools, the simplest way to get involved is to contact the responsible manager and ask how you can help. Or you may wish to encourage management to expand current efforts or move in new directions.

If your company has not yet joined the tide of school-business cooperation, you have a great opportunity. You may be able to convince management to become active supporters of public schools, and then accomplish far more than you could acting alone. The time is certainly ripe. More and more American companies, even those that once expressed complete indifference to pre-college education, are now lining up to work with, and fund, projects in K-12 schools. For activities of some major corporations, see Appendix G.

Start with your direct superior and explain to him or her what you would like the company to do. Ask if your boss will accompany you in an appeal to top management. When you make your pitch, use the arguments in this book (see pages 4-12), but stress the classic approach to business leaders: self-interest. Your company's involvement in public education, after all, will help to guarantee a supply of educated workers, reduce the need for company programs to train workers in skills they should have learned in school, please employees whose children benefit from company-sponsored programs, and provide good will for the company among potential customers. Some forms of involvement can also mean tax breaks for the company.

If your company decides to get involved, staff can begin thinking about its role by reviewing the activities of other branches of the company and of other companies (see Appendix G), and by considering how to target its assistance. The National Alliance of Business categorizes school improvement strategies as operating on five levels of involvement:

Level 1: Policy. Business efforts to affect laws or regulations so as to change the overall direction of education systems; a coalition of businesses, for example, might lobby alongside leaders of the education community to change state laws about the distribution of state funds to urban schools or about the length of the school year.

Level 2: Systemic Educational Improvements. Business efforts to encourage and facilitate reforms throughout one or more public-school systems; for example, a chemical company might help to modernize the K-12 science curriculum or lead a community effort to define and measure progress concerning a school system's improvement goals.

Level 3: Management Assistance. Business assistance to schools in such areas as purchasing, maintenance of plant and equipment, computer technology, long-range planning, insurance, finance, accounting, organizational development, productivity, and public relations; for example, a corporation might loan a manager to the school system for an extended period of time or provide a team of experts to recommend energy efficiencies to the district.

Level 4: Teacher Training. Business participation in the school system's professional development programs for teachers; a pharmaceutical company, for example, might help science teachers update their knowledge and improve their skills at conducting hands-on activities in the classroom, or provide opportunities for teachers to work in company research facilities as summer interns.

Level 5: Classroom Activity. Business efforts to deliver improved instruction directly to students; for example, a company might give its employees release time for classroom presentations about their jobs or avocations, or provide for class visits to company facilities or opportunities for students to work as interns.

Many business leaders believe that they should concentrate their efforts at levels 1 and 2, where there is the greatest potential for systemic improvement. What's the point, they ask, of investing thousands of employee-hours working in the classroom if the school has no coherent improvement plan or if state regulations inhibit meaningful reform? Your company's man-agers may agree. Or, they may feel that the best way to build a productive relationship with educators is to begin at level 3, 4, or 5.

Your company's managers also need to decide what schools to assist. Will the company concentrate on a few schools or provide less intensive help to many? Does it want to help high schools, junior high schools, elementary schools, or all three? Management's natural inclination will be to help schools in the communities where company facilities are located and in those where most employees live. But for many corporations, this will mean helping the suburban schools that need it least. For public relations reasons, at least some efforts will probably have to be directed at these targets, but your company should also consider providing assistance to schools in the nearest city. And that raises the question of whether your company should act alone or in concert with other corporations or organizations.

To settle these and other questions, large companies will probably designate someone to be in charge of educational efforts. In the largest, most active corporations, this may be a full-time job, but in most companies it will become an added responsibility of someone in the community affairs or public affairs office.

The duties of this "director of education relations" are to gather pertinent information, set goals and objectives for company activities, coordinate current company programs, recommend new programs to management, implement new programs, and monitor progress toward objectives. Most of these tasks are familiar components of good management practice. But two aspects of the job — information gathering in a specialized field and interacting with school personnel — may present special challenges.

Information gathering means keeping informed about education developments throughout the country, keeping abreast of needs and reform activities in schools your company has decided to assist, and networking with educational associations and interest groups on the local, state, and perhaps even the national level. In practice, these duties will require the staff member to read education periodicals (at least the indispensable *Education Week*) and to meet with and gather data from principals of affected schools. Networking with education groups is more difficult, because there is no central registry of such organizations. The director will certainly want to contact state organizations representing school boards, teachers, and school administrators, local education foundations, if any, and local parent groups. He or she will also want to inquire about the existence of programs or groups sponsored by other corporations, universities, churches, or civic organizations.

In preparing to work with school administrators, a director of education relations should visit classrooms in schools your company hopes to assist, and attend meetings of the school board. The director needs to understand that school systems are bound by complicated state regulations, that school board members have political concerns relating to representation and election, and that some administrators are understandably threatened by talk of failure, crisis, and restructuring. Sally Norodick, a businesswoman active in education reform in Washington state, offers this advice: "Business needs to understand that educators have a great deal of insight about what needs to be done, and they should work in collaboration with educators rather than swooping in with answers or thinking it can be done the way they would do it in a business environment."[18]

For companies that decide against ambitious programs of support for education, there are ways to help schools from a distance. Some of these are:

> **Holding seminars and conferences for employees who are school board members or school board candidates**. Larger companies probably have school board members or potential members among their employees. Because quality board members are so important to school improvement, your company will be making a valuable contribution to education if it improves the managerial skills of current board members and encourages talented employees to run for their local boards. Your company's management would not conduct the meetings,

of course, since they have little expertise in the field. Instead, your management would arrange for seasoned board members and well-reputed school administrators to address its employees. Your state school boards association may be able to assist you in getting started.

Rallying employees to get involved in education. Your company could do for interested employees what this book is attempting to do for its readers: persuade them to get involved and provide assistance to get them started. Some corporations do this by running in-house advertising campaigns and holding school improvement seminars during lunch hours. Attendees hear from educators, legislators, and reform advocates, and receive packets of information to help them take initial steps in their communities. Other large companies offer flexible hours and flexible leave policies for employees who want to become more involved in schools. Corporations may also back up their encouragement with commitments of financial support to resulting coalitions or organizations, such as local education foundations.

Rallying the public to get involved in education. Corporations have unique abilities in marketing. Who better to lead efforts to convince talented citizens to run for school board positions, to get out the vote, and to market the need for and dimensions of educational improvement in your state?

Making corporate donations to K-12 schools. Many companies have corporate giving programs, but exclude schools from them. Why? Because schools are funded by tax dollars and corporate giving programs traditionally have restricted their largesse to private non-profits. And because many companies have felt that post-secondary education is more important to their interests. More and more companies, though, including some of the largest in the country, are coming to realize that public schools merit their support and are changing their policy to permit donations at that level.

Changing matching gift policies to include public schools. Over 1,000 companies in America have matching gift programs. That is, they match contributions that their employees make to certain types of charitable organization. Usually, the company matches donations dollar for dollar, but some double or even triple their workers' gifts. Here, too, many companies restrict their matching gifts programs to post-secondary or to private schools. But recent years have seen a trend to extend programs to public schools. If your company has a matching gifts program (your personnel office can tell you), ask if it matches gifts to public schools. If not, ask your management to consider changing its policies. You might want to support your argument by citing other companies, especially those in your area, that have such policies. To find out what other companies do, consult *Matching Gift Details*, an annual publication of the Council for the Advancement and Support of Education (CASE).

Starting a matching gift program. If your company does not have a matching gift program, you could try to convince management to start one. The size of your company doesn't matter; firms with as few as four employees have such programs. Before you talk to your boss, though, get some free, expert advice from CASE's National Clearinghouse for Corporate Matching Gift Information (see Resources section for telephone number and details). Clearinghouse personnel will send you pamphlets you can use in preparing your sales pitch and may be willing to discuss the topic directly with your company's managers.

Lobbying on behalf of education reform. Corporations generally have the capacity to lobby strongly for state and national legislative action in support of their business interests. Your company's lobbyists could also weigh in on behalf of education reform. This kind of support is often essential to regulatory or statutory change, because legislators cannot dismiss business leaders as they sometimes do educators. If your company decides to take this route, it will need to know what education bills are before the state and national legislatures and decide which ones are worthy of support. The National Alliance of Business can be helpful in both regards (see Resources section).

Hire a Student

High-school students who work up to ten hours a week at income-producing jobs do better in school than their non-working peers.[19] They learn responsibility and self-discipline, and they gain a measure of self-respect. For most students, the money gives them a degree of independence they would not otherwise have and, in some homes, it makes a real difference in how the family as a whole manages.

If you do hire students, however, keep in mind that working too many hours (more than ten per week) results in sleepy teens and slipping grades. Students who work more than twenty hours each week have grade-point averages almost a half point below those of students who work fewer hours. These students also miss out on athletics and other after-school activities.

Fortunate students have good bosses — supervisors who craft schedules around their classes, athletic practices, and school events, and who motivate student employees to do well in school. For instance, McDonald's restaurants in Baton Rouge, Louisiana pay an extra 15 cents an hour to students who carry a 3.0 or better grade-point average.

There are other kinds of students who have a critical need for employment. They are physically, mentally, or emotionally handicapped students taking part in work-preparation programs conducted by their schools. School staff are generally available to help such students adjust to the workplace and assist in on-the-job training. Employers find that these young people tend to be excellent employees. While the tasks they can perform depend upon their handicapping condition, given the right circumstances, they may even outperform "normal" workers. Many develop an intense devotion to their jobs. Their presence is also valuable to fellow-workers, who get a new perspective on the handicapped and their very real abilities. Handicapped students have become successful employees of hospitals, restaurants, machine-tool companies, libraries, toy stores, publishing firms, bakeries, and pharmaceutical manufacturers, to name just a few. It's a win-win situation — students gain job skills and experience, employers gain good workers.

If you would like to hire a student, but do not know any suitable young people, call the school district or high-school office to inquire about students who want to work. In some cases, administrators or guidance counselors will already have names of potential employees for you; in others, they will post a sign about your needs.

Attend School Board Meetings and Public Hearings

You and your neighbors can demonstrate your community's concern for quality education by regularly attending school board meetings, public hearings and, where permitted, board subcommittee meetings. A watched board is a careful board; its members know that the public feels what they do is important enough to monitor and that their actions must pass public scrutiny. Check your local newspaper or call your board of education office to find out when board meetings are scheduled.

In addition, some organizations, such as the League of Women Voters and the American Association of University Women (AAUW), hold discussions on general topics related to public education or on specific state and local issues. In some school districts, the League, AAUW, Jaycees, Chamber of Commerce, local Democratic and Republican Committees, and other community groups regularly review proposed school budgets and make recommendations to the board of education. They also hold hearings where school board candidates are asked to speak and answer questions. Attending some of these meetings can give you a good idea of the issues facing the district and provide a forum for you to express your opinions.

Public Meetings

Most boards provide opportunities at their public meetings for citizen input on specific agenda items and general concerns. Some states (see table on the following page) require boards of education to permit either public input at meetings or some other form of participation in board decision-making. Even if your state is not one of these, check your local district's policy manual or ask a board member or district administrator how the board handles public input. Some require you to register an advance request to speak at a public meeting; others hold open forums at the beginning or end of meetings.

States With Laws Guaranteeing the Public's Right to Speak
California
Hawaii
Illinois
Michigan
Montana
Nebraska
Utah (guaranteed under state constitution)
Vermont
West Virginia
Wyoming
District of Columbia

Source: Beyond the Open Door, *National
Committee for Citizens in Education, 1989.*

It may be useful, depending on where you are and what the
situation is, to learn a bit about parliamentary procedure before you
attend a board meeting. School boards in small towns and rural
areas often operate informally; those in larger communities tend to
be more formal. Also, when there is only a handful of people in the
audience, a board is likely to approach public input more casually
than when the room is filled with people who are hot about an issue
and eager to have their say. When formal rules of procedure are
invoked, the governing guide is often Robert's Rules of Order.
(General Robert's codification of parliamentary rules isn't the only
one, however. *Parliamentary Procedure at a Glance* by O. Garfield
Jones, Hawthorn Books, Inc., New York, 1971, offers a different
approach to the same rules and is particularly easy to use. Your
library should have a copy of one or the other.) If you have some
understanding of how a group arrives at decisions under parliamentary procedures — how motions are made, modified, and voted on,
for instance — you will be better able to follow what is going on
during a meeting, more likely to address your concerns to the board
at appropriate points in the process, and less likely to be intimidated
by opponents who try to use procedural rules against you.

When you do speak before the board, try to keep your remarks as
brief and to the point as possible. Board meetings are often very
lengthy, and board members, like everyone else, can get weary and
inattentive after a while. If you think a longer explanation is neces-

sary, write a preliminary or follow-up letter to the board. In any case, ask the board to respond to your concern either in writing or at a specific board meeting. A good board will agree to your request, but if yours fails to do so, keep asking until you get results. Squeaky wheels really do get attention.

Remember, however, that a board of education's main function is to establish policy for the district as a whole. If your issue concerns only one school in the district, the best place to address it is in the principal's office. Failing there, your next step is to go to the district superintendent. Only as a last resort do you take that kind of problem to the board. This is especially true if your concern is about a particular child.

For more information about how school boards function, see pages 163-164.

Public Hearings and Committee Meetings

Public hearings are often held before voters are presented with annual budgets and before the public is asked to approve the issuance of bonds to pay for construction projects. Holding a hearing in these circumstances is often a state requirement. Less often, public hearings are held in situations where considerable public interest and controversy are likely. A board might hold a public hearing when it is considering changes to the district's sports program, for instance, or deciding whether to close a school.

The purpose of hearings is to provide information and to hear what the public has to say about an issue. You can use these occasions to ask questions and state your opinions.

Boards of education are rarely able to accomplish all their work in one or two meetings a month. To handle the workload, some boards establish committees to review issues and proposals related to specific areas (buildings and grounds, curriculum, staffing, textbook selection, budgeting, contract negotiations, etc.) and make recommendations to the full board. Other boards operate as a board-of-the-whole, but hold work sessions in addition to public meetings; formal action can legally take place only at public meetings, but much important preparatory work goes on in work sessions. Some boards welcome the public at committee meetings and work sessions, but may not allow them to speak.

What Boards Talk About

When you attend board meetings, you can usually expect to hear discussions about:

textbooks to be approved for use

staff to be hired

staff to be fired (although discussions about individual
   performance will probably take place in closed session)

maintenance projects — planned or underway

problems with buses and bus schedules

suspensions and (rarely) expulsions of students (most
   substantive discussions will take place behind closed
   doors; what you will witness is the final action taken)

approval or rejection of employee contracts (negotiations
   are private)

curriculum changes

staffing changes

special education programs

test results

bills to be approved for payment

budget proposals

Of course, not every topic will appear on the agenda of each meeting, but over the course of a year you will hear discussions about each of these and many other topics as well. If your district is planning to construct new buildings, for instance, you can expect to listen to hours of talk about architects and builders and bond issues.

Sometimes boards get swamped by minutia and lose sight of the fact that they are supposed to be policy-making bodies. When that happens, even the hardiest board-watchers become bored-watchers. If you experience this, try asking the board president or secretary to place topics of greatest interest to the public at the top of the agenda. Also, if your board isn't spending at least part of each meeting listening to teachers and other staff talk about their instructional programs, suggest that they do so.

Join a Parent-Teacher Group

Everyone has heard of PTAs, but most people don't realize that parent-teacher groups are open to those who are neither parents nor teachers. Indeed, effective organizations are always on the lookout for "new blood," since parents tend to move on when their children do. Developing new leadership is critical to the group's continued existence. Because parent-teacher groups are an easy way to get involved in the life of a local school, you might consider joining one, even if you no longer have (or never had) children in attendance there.

Parent-teacher groups go by various names: Parent-Teacher Association (PTA), Parent-Teacher Organization (PTO), and Home and School Committee are some of the common ones. The difference between a PTA and the others is that PTAs are affiliated with state and national organizations, while the others usually are not. The advantage of belonging to a larger network is that the local group can reach out to its parent organization for information and support. State and national levels also represent local interests at higher levels of government, and offer a forum for local members to become involved in broader educational issues.

Every parent-teacher group is unique in that each has developed its own ideas about how it should be involved in the school. New members should consider whether a group is devoted primarily to socializing (mainly chitchat and little substance at meetings), is involved mainly in fundraising (it holds lots of bake sales), or is active in school decision-making (the group is consulted on important decisions and involved, where appropriate, in implementing them). Either of the last two can be helpful to the school, but you'll probably feel more comfortable in one setting or the other.

Fundraising is a time-honored tradition of parent-teacher groups. Bake sales have funded a great deal of school equipment over the years. Some of these efforts — book fairs, for instance — provide not only extra dollars but educational nourishment as well.

Sometimes, fundraising by a parent group makes a significant difference in the quality of education provided to the children in the school. Take Public School 40 in New York City, for instance. In 1991, the parent group there raised enough money to pay for the salaries of a music teacher and a classroom aide (neither of whom would have been hired otherwise), art supplies, and a science program, and had enough left to set aside for a planned computer center. To get it, they sponsored an auction, a magic show, a crafts fair, a candy and gift-wrap sale, an Easter and Passover candy sale, a rock 'n roll dance for students, and a buffet dinner with dishes donated by parents.[20] That's enough to make even the hardiest parent beg for mercy, but they did it because their children's education would have suffered otherwise.

But if your school is not one that has to depend on fundraising for basic needs, perhaps some of the group's energy can be directed toward doing other things with and for the school. Here are some ideas you might offer:

- Establish an outreach program that encourages parents to become involved in the school and in their children's learning, and that draws community members into the life of the school. Included could be a hospitality committee or a host family program to greet families who are new to the community, especially those who are non-English speaking.

- Set up an information program. This might include regular or occasional programs, with presentations by school officials, teachers, parents, and other community members, and with discussions about aspects of the school's curriculum and instruction, its evaluation and reporting systems, its homework and discipline policies, test results, or school improvement plans. The program could also include a school newsletter with articles about the same topics, and the submission of articles about the school to local newspapers.

- Identify, with the help of school staff, the school's most pressing problem, then develop strategies to resolve it. The problem should be one of some substance and one that everyone feels committed to working on. Once it is taken care of, use the same procedure to identify and address other concerns.

- Encourage the principal to establish a citizen advisory committee to help prepare the school's improvement plans or, better yet, to form a school-site council with real decision-making authority.

You can also consider some of the activities more commonly associated with local education foundations (see pages 101-110). Some of these suggestions go well beyond the traditional parent-teacher group activities, so you might meet some resistance. If your purpose in joining such a group is to have some influence on a particular school and the group you've chosen does not see its role in this way, you have several choices: you can abandon it for a more activist group (if one exists), you can start your own group (for a discussion of how to become a citizen advocate, see pages 111-121), or you can try to get the group to change.

If you choose the latter, one thing you might do first is find some kindred spirits — there are bound to be some — and talk about what you would like the group to become. Then nibble around the edges, encouraging incremental changes in how the group operates. Work to get some like-minded members into leadership positions. Volunteer to lead activities (when you're in charge, people will let you do things pretty much your own way). Given time, and some finesse on your part, you can get things done.

Participate in Election and Budget Campaigns

Getting the word out to voters is a challenge. Anyone who has run a political campaign in a district of any size can tell you how much effort it requires and how much help is always needed. There are two different types of campaigns you can get involved in — campaigns for public office and campaigns for budget, bond, or other tax levy referenda.

Election Campaigns

Making sure the "right" people are in positions to influence critical school decisions is one of the best ways to advance quality education. If yours is a district with direct election of board members, you might want to help the most qualified people — and those who agree with your views — get elected to the board (for determining who is most qualified, see pages 19-23). If school board members are appointed, you will need to make sure their appointers have the best interests of the schools at heart. In either case, once you have determined the best candidate or candidates, the next level of involvement is to volunteer your time to help their campaign. Also, keep in mind that you do not have to be a voter in a district in order to work on an election campaign. So if you are concerned about the quality of education in a community other than your own, this is a good way to help.

Budget and Bond Campaigns

Budget campaigns and bond referenda are often poorly understood (for information about how budgets are prepared, see pages 171-174; for information about bond issues, see pages 22-23), yet they can sometimes become heated. There are always those who will oppose anything that calls for additional taxes, of course, but there are also situations where individuals and groups have concerns about particular aspects of a budget or a building program. They may think teachers or administrators are being paid too much or that there are more of them than needed; they may want more money from the district's "rainy day" fund (free appropriations balance) to be used to hold down tax rates; they may object to the inclusion of a swimming pool in the plans for a new high school. On the other side, there are automatic "yes" votes by those who feel that "We have to support our kids" and from groups that coalesce in support of maintaining current courses and services, strengthening special education, or putting a new roof on a school. Whatever the issue, sides form and a battle begins. Municipal officials often take a stand (usually tilted toward holding down taxes), community organizations may become involved, and the local newspaper gets flooded with letters to the editor. You, too, can influence the outcome by campaigning for your point of view.

What You Can Do

Whether you want to help out in a school board election or in a budget or bond referendum, there are plenty of time-tested ways to campaign for your position:

- Talk to your neighbors and friends to influence their thinking and find out who would like to work with you. One way to do this is by organizing neighborhood "coffees" or cocktail parties where candidates or advocates of your position on a budget or bond referendum can make presentations and answer questions.

- Write letters to local newspapers (don't forget the give-away kind) explaining your position and the rationale for it.

- Attend and support your candidate at "candidates nights;" attend and support your views at any budget or bond referendum hearings held by the school district.

- Assist in or make presentations at meetings of PTA and other community organizations, such as Rotary, the Chamber of Commerce, and the League of Women Voters. Pay particular attention to senior citizen groups — they tend to vote out of proportion to their numbers — and they usually, but not always, oppose increased spending.

- Solicit contributions for ads, brochures, flyers, and other components of your campaign.

- Go door-to-door, alone or with friends, explaining your views. The best time to catch people at home is early weekday evenings and weekend afternoons.
- Print and distribute flyers, door-to-door (you may need a municipal permit) or at booths set up in shopping centers (get center manager permission first) or other commercial areas (a municipal permit may be required here also).
- Make posters and signs for store windows and yards.
- Write speeches, press releases, and other materials for your candidate or your position on the budget or bond referendum.
- Purchase advertising space in local newspapers, or time on radio and television stations.
- Organize a telephone "get-out-the-vote" campaign to first identify supporters and then, on election day, remind them to go to the polls.
- Arrange transportation to the polls for senior and handicapped citizens who are supporting your cause.
- Serve as a poll watcher to monitor voting activity and to check off names of supporters as they come to vote (and feed names of those who have not voted to the get-out-the-vote telephone squad).

But none of this applies to you, you say, because your community does not get to vote on school board members, school budgets, or decisions about capital outlays. Your mayor, or a county executive, appoints your school board. And financial decisions are made by municipal or county officials, a board of school finance (usually made up of municipal and school officials), or state legislators. So you don't have the opportunity to participate in election campaigns for better schools.

Of course you do! Voters in your community still have an indirect say about important educational matters. So shift your focus and get active in election campaigns for the appropriate municipal, county, and state officials. Maybe you can serve to remind your whole community that a political candidate's views and record on education should be one of the most important factors in the election. And once the politicians are in office, rally your community to keep pressure on them to "do the right thing" for your public schools.

Join or Form a Booster Club

School athletic teams, which in many towns are a focus of community pride, have long benefited from community booster clubs. Club members raise funds for needed equipment, form cheering sections at athletic events, and acknowledge, through awards and dinners, the athletic achievements of youngsters. With the tightening of many school budgets, these clubs are more important than ever. Less popular sports, such as field hockey and gymnastics, and women's sports programs may be threatened with cuts. And clubs can speak out for intramural as well as interscholastic sports.

While it is important to foster the lessons that sports give to young people, it's equally valuable to give kids the message that academics count. You may have seen bumper stickers announcing "My child made such and such a school's honor roll." Imagine the impact if that kind of pride could be extended to the whole school, if a community would celebrate the academic achievements of the student body just as it does the athletic prowess of a winning team.

One way to do this is to form a booster organization to support academic achievement, similar to the ones for athletics. These booster club members can help improve communication between the school, parents, and the community by publicizing student efforts and successes in local newspapers, and club and church bulletins. They can motivate students by recognizing and rewarding their achievements — even hold annual academic awards banquets, just like the ones for athletic achievement. The club could help raise funds for enrichment materials for classroom use, for activities outside the normal budget (an SAT coaching program, for instance), or for college scholarships. And it could serve as an organized resource of talent and energy to support school staff.

Another approach would be to join forces with the school's athletic booster club. Perhaps that organization could be expanded to include scholars as well as athletes (or at least give special honor to scholar-athletes). Or joint activities might be held, making athletics and scholarship equally important in building school pride.

Serve As a Bridge Between the Schools and the Community

Do you have a job that puts you in frequent touch with residents of a community? Are you, perhaps, a

shop owner or clerk
barber or hairdresser
nurse or physician
pharmacist
member of the clergy
real estate agent
mail deliverer
police officer
municipal clerk
gas station attendant
restaurant owner or worker?

If you are, you can play a unique role in the public schools: that of school communicator. The school district where you work (it doesn't have to be the one where you live) may have a program where people like you are invited to visit schools periodically for discussions about what is happening in the district. The purpose is to keep a corps of communicators up-to-date on school achievements and problems, so they can pass on information to other members of the community. If a crisis or a particularly thorny problem comes up, school communicators are called immediately so they can provide the public with facts and help to head off rumors and innuendo. At the same time, school communicators serve as the district's windows to the community, helping school personnel understand concerns and perceptions parents and citizens have regarding the schools.

If your school or school district has this kind of program, your participation will be welcomed — the more the better when it comes to communicators. Call the district's public relations officer (if there is one) or the superintendent or the principal from your local school to find out if such a program exists. If not, you could use the same phone call to suggest one be started. You might even volunteer to help get it going. Contact the National School Public Relations Association, 1501 Lee Highway, Arlington, VA 22209 (703/528-5840) for information.

Become a Mentor or Establish a Mentoring Program

Mentoring is a special form of volunteering — one that is gaining more attention as a way to address the problems of youth who are at risk of school failure and dropping out. More than just tutoring, the goal of mentoring is to help youngsters gain the skills and self-esteem necessary to create positive futures for themselves. Mentors act as role models, coaches, and advisors. Some mentoring programs focus on specific groups — young black males, children from disadvantaged homes, fatherless boys, or pregnant students, for instance. Others are open to all youngsters experiencing academic or social difficulties, and some offer mentoring to any student who wants it. These programs focus primarily, but not exclusively, on adolescents, and not all of them are tied to public schools.

Mentors come from a wide variety of walks of life. Some are senior citizens, some are business people, some are college students. In a 1989 study, Public/Private Ventures of Philadelphia found more than 1,700 programs matching college students with at-risk youths. Anyone who has the interests of kids at heart (and enough time) can become someone's mentor.

Who Makes a Good Mentor?

Mentoring is an activity for you if you:

- Can devote four to six hours a week for at least a year to being with "your" young person;
- Have a reasonably easy time making new friends;
- Are not looking for quick results (attitudinal and behavioral changes happen slowly);
- Are comfortable with who you are, but don't necessarily expect others to conform to your values, attitudes, and ideas;
- Have strong listening skills;
- Can set appropriate limits with children;
- Do not abuse alcohol or drugs;
- Are open to supervision;

- Keep your commitments;
- Know how to constructively manage anger — your own and that of others; and
- Possess the maturity to let go when a relationship doesn't pan out or has reached its limits or goals.

The trick is to find a mentoring program that will do a good job of pairing you with a young person with whom you can establish a positive relationship.

How You Can Become a Mentor

If mentoring is your cup of tea, contact a mentoring program that operates after-school programs in your area, such as Big Brothers/Big Sisters (for other possible sponsors, look under "Youth Organizations" in the yellow pages of your telephone book). If you work for a major corporation, ask your personnel office if the company is involved in mentoring. Or, to see if your school district participates in such a program, call the district office or individual middle and high schools. In any case, talk with the program coordinators about the nature and goals of their programs. Are they primarily interested in developing academic skills, for instance? Or do they have broader aims? What kind of kids are involved in the program? Boys? Girls? What are their ages? Typical home environments? What are the expectations for mentors? How long has the program been in existence? How successful has it been? By what criteria? Before you commit to any program, be sure it is well run and meets your needs and desires. Talking with some mentors and, if possible, some students is a good idea (see pages 34-35 for more ideas).

Tips for the New Mentor

Here are some suggestions for making your mentoring efforts successful:

- Be aware that your partner is probably as uncertain about this new situation as you are and might even feel insulted that he or she is thought to need a mentor;

- Be aware that adolescence is a time when children are learning independence; they think they are omnipotent, so don't take their self-centeredness and resistance to perceived authority personally;

- Introduce yourself by talking about your family, your interests, your hobbies, etc.; ask your partner about the same things;

- Plan some activities for each of your meetings; try to find something that will absorb the energies of both of you;

- Don't try to provide solutions for your partner's problems — the point is for your partner to develop solutions for him- or herself;

- Keep appointments; be on time; stay in contact during school vacations;

- Never break the confidentiality of your partner's disclosures to you without his or her prior approval, unless you fear physical harm to him or her or to others;

- Be patient. Building a relationship takes time. Your partner may test your commitment from time to time until trust is firmly established.

And remember, what you give, you'll get back — maybe not today or even in the short run, but eventually the good you do will be repaid in kind.

How You Can Start a Mentoring Program

If your community has no mentoring program, you can organize one. Putting together a mentoring program is similar to creating any other kind of school volunteer program (see pages 37-40), with one major difference. If your program is to operate outside the school building or other common meeting place (and most mentoring programs do: in a home, at a sports event, in a museum), you must set up a mentor screening process for the protection of the children involved. This screening should include face-to-face interviews, home visits, and reference checks (including driving and criminal record checks, where legally permissible). You will want to institute a careful monitoring system, as well. It may be worth your while to work with a national or regional program in developing your screening process or joining your program with theirs. For help in starting a mentoring program, contact the National Mentoring Working Group (see Resources section).

Mentor training is very important and so is careful matching of mentors and students. The National Mentoring Working Group suggests that, when making assignments, you consider such factors as:

Languages spoken
Interests
Life experiences
Temperament
Gender
Age
Ethnic and cultural backgrounds

In general, mentoring programs try to match partners as closely as possible. Youngsters are more likely to make role models of adults who share their cultural background and gender. With skilled leadership, mentoring programs can grow quickly and branch out to provide other forms of support to students.

The organization called Philadelphia Futures serves as a inspiring example of how rapidly mentoring programs can begin to make a difference in their communities. Founded in 1989 by Marciene Mattleman, a former Temple University professor and executive director of the Philadelphia Mayor's Commission on Literacy, the group has since recruited, trained, and placed over 2,150 mentors. And because its focus is on preparing students for college education, Philadelphia Futures went much further. It solicited $948,000 in scholarship funds through its Sponsor-A-Scholar program, raised another $276,000 for achievement and incentive prizes for students, presented workshops on colleges and financial aid to 8,200 students, organized career days, arranged college visits, established a financial aid hotline, and distributed 95,000 copies of its annual guide to colleges and financial aid. Small wonder that Philadelphia Mayor Edward Rendell hails Philadelphia Futures as a "wonderful educational resource" that is "increasing the possibilities for our young people to succeed."

Like establishing any other volunteer program, getting an effective mentoring program up and running is no easy task. It requires dedication, stamina, and a knack for getting people to join your efforts. One of the rewards for exerting the extra effort it takes to get a mentoring program started, however, is the knowledge that once the program takes on a life of its own, it will go on making an impact on kid's lives even after you are no longer part of it. You will have left a legacy to the children of your community.

Serve on an Advisory Committee

When a school district wants to get community opinion about an issue or resolve a problem, it frequently relies on community advisory committees. These committees, made up of parents, community leaders, business representatives, and district staff members, may be ad hoc or standing committees. Ad hoc advisory committees, those that will disband as soon as they accomplish their specific responsibility, might be charged with:

> recommending one or more candidates for a principalship or the superintendency;
> recommending solutions to a school facilities problem;
> suggesting ways to reduce student violence;
> deciding whether to close a school and, if so, which one;
> deciding whether to regionalize, or merely cooperate with neighboring school districts;
> studying alternatives to ability grouping;
> determining the need for after-school programs;
> developing a multicultural curriculum;
> investigating requests to remove books from a school library; or
> determining the content of the sexuality education curriculum.

Standing, or permanent, committees will have an ongoing mission, such as:

> reviewing proposals for curriculum changes;
> monitoring and supporting the district's athletic program;
> advising the administration about educational uses of new technologies;
> reviewing proposed textbook adoptions;
> addressing concerns of racial or ethnic minorities;
> examining budget proposals;
> advising a youth services program; or
> providing ongoing advice to a particular principal.

Some districts rely heavily on advisory committees, and you may be asked to serve on one. The likelihood of being chosen is higher if you have demonstrated your interest in the schools by attending board of education meetings or by being active in a parent or parent-teacher group. Members of the clergy, by virtue of their prominence in the community, are also likely to be selected, as are local business people and leaders of community organizations, whether they live in the community or not.

But don't wait to be appointed — volunteer your services. Call the district office and ask what committees now exist and how you can submit your name for consideration. Some districts maintain a list of volunteers and their interests, so that when an advisory committee is needed on a particular issue, administrators can quickly enlist those who have expressed interest, add some appointees, and give the group its charge.

Remember, too, that there are ways to help an advisory committee without being a member. You may be able to assist by doing research, entering data, interviewing experts, writing reports, and the like.

Some individual schools also use committees to help make decisions. Frequently, these are made up of parents of students in the school and some of the school's teachers, but sometimes (especially if the principal is asked) other community members are also welcome to join. As with district-level committees, school advisory committees can be standing or ad hoc.

As a member of an advisory committee, you can have a real influence on what happens in your district. Are you concerned about your district's spending priorities? Then get on a budget review committee and help shape its recommendations. Don't worry about not having an accounting background; the district needs input from ordinary citizens just like you.

The most common standing committee in a school is the principal's advisory council. Some principals make good use of these committees. They use them as their windows to the school community, looking for concerns about their schools and ideas for how to improve them. Keep in mind, however, that these are advisory committees, not decision-making bodies. If you are interested in making decisions, read about serving on a school council (see pages 70-73).

Not all suggestions of advisory committees are heeded, even by the best of principals, and less capable principals may ignore much of the advice given. Unfortunately, that can also be the case with district-wide committees. Boards and superintendents have been known to put together committees just "for show," so before you volunteer for or accept appointment to a committee, ask some questions of the person in charge of it:

- What is the purpose of the committee?

- How much time will be required of committee members? How often will they be meeting? Will there be work to do between meetings?

- What is the committee's deadline for reporting? Are interim reports expected?

- If the topic is controversial, how well represented is the entire spectrum of community opinion?

- How much authority does the committee have? Have the board, superintendent, or principal indicated they expect to abide by the committee's decisions or are they planning to take its recommendations under consideration? What areas is the committee not authorized to get into?

These are important questions, but getting clear answers is not always easy. However, to avoid overstepping boundaries — which may make people angry — and to reduce the chance of false expectations and hurt feelings, these issues should be addressed. You need to feel comfortable about the charge to the committee and your role in its deliberations. Once you are satisfied that this committee is one where you can make a contribution and that its conclusions will be put to good use, you can devote yourself to helping it hold productive discussions and arrive at intelligent decisions. Here are some ways you can do that:[21]

- Come prepared to talk about agenda items. If everyone does his or her homework, meetings will be more efficient and decisions more effective. Seek input into the development of the agenda so that important items are addressed first.

- Listen carefully to what others say. Try to understand their point of view. See if you can learn something from them.

- If you don't understand what is being said, say so. Ask for examples and illustrations.

- Join the discussion. Don't wait to be called on. Say what you think. Other committee members need to know your thoughts on the subject.

- Don't speak so long — or so often — that others do not have a chance to speak.

- Disagree when necessary, but keep it friendly. State why you hold your opinions, but don't insist on their being accepted by others.

- Never argue a point of fact. It's a waste of time. Look up the answer or have someone do it for the next meeting.

Serving on an advisory committee can be very informative and a lot of fun. You'll meet people whose interests are the same as yours. If it is a well-run committee, you'll also come away from the experience with a sense of having accomplished something important for the students in your school district.

Serve on a School Council

More and more schools and school districts are moving toward establishing a school-based form of management. Chicago, for instance, now has councils governing every school. Under this system, many decisions affecting a school that were previously made by the board of education and central office administrators are made by a group consisting of the principal, representatives of the school's professional and support staff, parents, other members of the public, and, sometimes, students.

Unlike advisory committees, school or school-site councils do more than recommend. They have authority to make decisions. The extent of this authority varies from state to state and district to district, but it can include the power to hire and dismiss staff, establish curricula, evaluate results, develop plans for improving the school, plan training programs for staff, and determine budgets.

Usually, school district budgets lump together, by category, the amounts to be spent by all the schools. Teachers' salaries, for instance, fall under the heading of Instruction and are not broken out school by school (for background on school budgets, see pages 171-174). Where school councils are given the authority to develop school budgets, however, the board of education and district administration determine how much in each category would normally be spent on behalf of a school and allocate some or all of it to the school's council. The council then determines, within certain parameters, how it wants to use it. If, for instance, the council can purchase heating fuel at a lower cost or, through energy conservation measures, spend less than expected for fuel, the council can use the savings for other things. They cannot, however, keep the school at unsafe or uncomfortable temperatures to achieve savings, nor can they spend money in frivolous or illegal ways.

The role of the board and central administration under school-based management is to establish district-wide goals and objectives, review and approve school improvement plans, negotiate collective bargaining agreements, coordinate the purchase of supplies and equipment, provide assistance to the school, and evaluate school outcomes in relation to district goals. A smaller central office staff can be one result of an effective school-based management approach.

Serving on a school council, if your district has them, will give you an opportunity to make a substantial difference in that school. Typically, council members are involved in:

> collecting and analyzing information about conditions in the school
>
> setting priorities for school improvement
>
> developing school improvement plans
>
> monitoring implementation of planned activities
>
> setting up task groups to address school-wide issues
>
> reviewing task group reports
>
> making program and policy recommendations to the central office and board of education
>
> making reports to staff, central office, school board, and community
>
> evaluating achievements of the school and the council.

In schools where budget-making authority rests with the council, members are also involved with determining spending priorities, seeking creative ways to stretch available dollars, and monitoring expenditures.

Council members are expected to:[22]

> attend council meetings
>
> act as a link between the council and staff, parents, and community
>
> assume various roles on the council to assure that proposed objectives are achieved
>
> contribute to the group and help members function as a team.

Councils are typically made up of 10 to 25 members, and they tend to meet monthly, although some activities require additional time.

For more information on school-based management, see pages 149-150.

How to Get on a Council

Council members are primarily drawn from three sources: parents of children in the school, school staff members, and other community members. There usually are no other qualifications necessary, but if you want to serve on a council, you will need to make yourself known to those who do the selecting. The best way to do this is to become active in the school — by volunteering there or by involving yourself in a school-related group. If you hold a position of respect in the community, you may find yourself being sought out. If you don't live in the community, it is unlikely you will be asked to serve, unless you have strong ties of some kind.

Some councils are appointed — by the principal, constituent groups (such as teachers or the parent-teacher organization), or both. If this is the case in your school, you can improve your chances of being asked to serve by seeking out those who make the appointments and expressing your interest.

Other districts rely on volunteers, so in these you only have to put your name forward. Allentown, Pennsylvania's ACCORD Councils, for instance, have the following clause in their bylaws:

> Selection for membership shall be through volunteers. In the event there are more parent/community representative volunteers than there are vacant seats, a lottery shall be held. In the event there are more staff member volunteers than are needed, elections shall be held.

ACCORD councils are made up of:
   three parents and one community representative, with one
      vote each
   three professional staff representatives, with one vote each
   one support staff representative, with one vote
   one facilitator (a central office staff person), with no vote
   the building principal, with one vote
   one open chair position (for anyone wishing to attend and
      participate in a council meeting), with no vote

You will note that there are two ways, under this system, that non-parents can be part of a council: as the one community representative or by filling the open chair.

School improvement councils in South Carolina use a third method — election. By statute, a minimum of two parents must be elected by the parents of students in the school, two teachers elected by their colleagues in the school, and two students (in schools serving grades nine and above) elected by their fellow students. If your school uses this or a similar method, and you have children in the school, you may have to campaign for a seat. South Carolina does provide for an alternative method, however. Principals are permitted to appoint others to their councils, provided they do not number more than one-third of the membership. This allows interested non-parents to hold seats.

Characteristics of Effective Councils

Councils that work well share a common set of characteristics. If you are interested in joining a council, here are some questions you may want to ask in order to judge its effectiveness:

- Is it truly representative? Does the selection process guarantee it? Are potential candidates recruited from different segments of the community? If elections are held, is there also a mechanism for balancing the group in terms of race, sex, geography, and other variables? Are task forces or ad hoc committees created to involve more people in the work of the council and to ensure greater representation?

- Does it have a clear sense of purpose? Are yearly goals and objectives set? Do they match the school's needs? Do council members feel they have accomplished something worthwhile at the end of the school year?

- Are roles and responsibilities well defined? Is each council member aware of his/her responsibilities? Are they given a thorough orientation, and is training provided in effective school practices and group dynamics?

- Is the group organized for action? Does the council meet regularly, for instance? Do meetings last for at least an hour and a half to two hours, so there is sufficient time to accomplish the complex process of assessing, planning, and monitoring? Is there a clear agenda for each meeting? Is the chairperson elected by council members rather than appointed by the principal? Do members feel that council meetings are worth their personal time and effort?

- Does the council evaluate its own processes and procedures in addition to evaluating its effectiveness in improving the school?

Serving on a school council is like serving on an advisory committee, only with greater responsibilities. The rewards are similar — an opportunity to make new friends and the satisfaction of doing something important.

Serve on a School Board

Membership on a school board, or board of education, can be one of the most challenging and satisfying ways to serve your community and its children. For some, it is also an entry into the political life of the community. One of its rewards is being in on what is happening in the community and its schools. People will look to you for information; they'll also expect you to look out for their interests. Serving on a board is a big, and important, job — one not to be taken lightly.

The duties of school board members generally include:

- appointing, evaluating, determining salary and, when necessary, dismissing the district superintendent of schools;
- establishing district goals and plans (with input from the community and staff);
- evaluating results of district plans;
- formulating policy for managing schools and school properties;
- hiring, evaluating, dismissing, and disciplining staff (according to collective bargaining agreements and tenure statutes, if any);
- enforcing state regulations;
- approving textbooks (according to state guidelines, if any);
- determining curricula (except for state-mandated courses of study);
- investigating and adjudicating appeals by staff members or students relating to board policies, including school expulsions; and
- budgeting (including, where permitted, submission of tax levy referenda to voters).

Boards and Their Superintendents

A school board has to work closely with the district's superintendent of schools. The superintendent's office is the administrative arm of the board and the board depends on its administration for the information it needs to make good decisions. All too often, boards and their superintendents find themselves at odds with one another. In fact, this is probably the most common problem boards have to face.

There is an inherent tension built into the relationship between a board and its superintendent. This tension can be positive if it leads to a balance between the different roles each has to play. Sometimes, however, it leads to struggles for power. In other cases, one or the other "gives up," or completely acquiesces to the other. This is just as unhealthy for a district as a power struggle is. A "lap dog" superintendent cannot provide the leadership a district needs; neither can a "rubber stamp" board provide the necessary oversight.

If you choose to serve on a board of education, it is important for you to understand the different roles each party must play and the balance of power between boards and superintendents. Even if you are just a "board watcher," knowing who should be making which kinds of decision can help you understand the process and where it may be going wrong. This chart illustrates the situations when each should be making decisions while the other serves in a supporting role:

	Goal Setting	Implementation	Evaluation
Board	Decision Maker	Advisor	Decision Maker
Superintendent	Advisor	Decision Maker	Advisor

The board is responsible for setting the district's goals and for determining how success or failure will be measured. The superintendent's role during this process is to provide information and advice. The implementation of programs to meet the goals, however, is the superintendent's responsibility. The board can provide guidance, but the day-to-day decisions belong to the superintendent and his or her staff. Making judgments about the success of those efforts, however, falls to the school board, with information supplied by the superintendent. Sometimes an issue won't divide clearly into these three categories, but making an effort to determine who has responsibility for what will result in better board/superintendent relations and a more effective school district.

Is This for You?

You don't have to have children in a district's schools to serve on its school board — in fact, many distinguished board members have never had children or have served long after their children graduated. Far more important is that you are well known and respected in your community. Legal requirements tend to be simple. All that is required in most states is that you be a citizen of the United States and a resident of your district. But there are other qualifications that are just as important. Before you decide to run for a board seat or try to get appointed to one, consider whether you have:

> sufficient time to devote to the job;
> an ability to listen to others with an open mind, and to get along with people with whom you disagree;
> the flexibility to change or negotiate your position on a subject;
> a degree of comfort in stating your opinions in an open forum;
> the ability to make decisions, sometimes promptly;
> the ability to withstand the pressure of public opinion, when necessary;
> a high degree of energy, especially if you also have to juggle the demands of a career and family;
> a reputation for integrity and a background that will bear public scrutiny.

How to Get on a Board

If you decide to run for the board in your local district, one of the first things you'll need to do is get a nominating petition, have it signed by the required number of registered voters in your district, and submit it to the board secretary or another designated official by a certain cut-off date. Petitions can be obtained at your board of education business office.

Then you will have to mount a campaign. In very small districts, this can amount to nothing more than telling your neighbors about your candidacy and submitting information to the local newspaper. At most, you might want to knock on a few doors and attend a "coffee" in your honor. In some districts, it's not uncommon for there to be the same number of candidates as there are vacant seats on the board, which means your election will be automatic (assuming no write-in candidate emerges). In larger districts, however, you may have to campaign seriously (for typical campaign activities, see pages 56-58). It will be a great advantage to you in such circumstances if you have already created a cadre of supporters through your work in the PTA, a civic group, your church, or a school advisory committee. If you'd like to run for the board next year, think about beginning your "campaign" now, by beginning to build a good reputation in such an organization. A good source of information about running for a school board is the book *How To Run a School Board Campaign and Win* by Cipora O. Schwartz.

Another way to get on an elected board, without having to conduct a formal election campaign, is to watch for board vacancies. You may be able to fill an unexpired term of office by appointment. You'll probably be able to serve only until the next election, but being an incumbent will then give you a leg up on your competition. To get the appointment, you'll have to submit an application and be interviewed by the school board or by a committee it has created for that purpose. It will help your cause if you are known and liked by at least some members of the board and can get respected members of your community to write letters to the board in your support.

If yours is a district with an appointed school board, in order to get a seat you'll have to make yourself known to those with appointing powers. Usually this happens through political party involvement, but sometimes it comes about through the intercession of others. If you want a seat and you know somebody who knows somebody, put the word out. You may just succeed.

The Upside and Downside of Being a Board Member

School board membership can be rewarding. It can also be stressful and frustrating. Important decisions affecting the lives of students and staff are in board members' hands, but their action is often restricted by financial limitations and state regulations. Effective board members know they have to represent the community's aspirations for its children and that, in so doing, they may not always please certain segments of the community or even their own colleagues. But they can also see, albeit sometimes not very clearly, the effects of their decisions on the quality of their schools.

Develop a Skills Directory

Picture a history teacher struggling to make World War II more vivid for students whose eyes glaze over as he lectures. Picture him consulting a booklet and finding names and telephone numbers of a survivor of the Dachau concentration camp; a veteran of the Normandy campaign; a woman who has kept letters and diaries her father wrote from an aircraft carrier in the Pacific; and a hobbyist who makes models of aircraft of the 1940s. Picture the teacher calling these people and arranging for them to make presentations to his students.

Now, picture yourself compiling the book the teacher found so valuable! It's a skills directory, a list of local resources available to assist teachers and school administrators.

When you think about it, isn't your area full of people who could enliven all kinds of classes in your schools? Here is only a sampling of the kinds of people who would be valuable:

- Artists and craftsmen to demonstrate their methods, help students design publications or stage sets, or merely talk about what their career or hobby has meant to them

- Experts and enthusiasts about any of the thousand and one things that can excite young people and make a class memorable: space travel, bears, Civil War weapons, mountain climbing, ancient coins, superconductivity, dinosaurs, women's rights, the Sistine Chapel, African drumming, the poems of Sylvia Plath

- Local businesspeople — bakers, bankers, newspaper editors, dry cleaners, farmers — willing to show a class of students through their facilities

- Local and county government officials to provide first-hand civics lessons or conduct tours of key facilities

- People fluent in French, Spanish, or German to give language students practice in conversational skills

- People to read to elementary students

- Photographers, whether professional or amateur, to advise a student photography club, teach darkroom skills, or help publicize school events

- Police, lawyers, and judges to explain the justice system
- Scientists to make presentations to science classes or advise science clubs (female and minority scientists can also provide needed role models)
- Someone who has traveled extensively in a foreign country who can enrich a geography or foreign-language lesson with slides, souvenirs, or stories
- Witnesses and participants in some of the great events of recent history, like the great depression, wars, anti-war protests, the civil rights movement, natural disasters
- Young engineers and other professionals to relate high-school lessons to college study and actual work experience

And, of course, your community is also full of people who could help the schools outside the classroom:

- Architects, building engineers, and construction experts to serve on buildings and grounds committees, assist with site selection for new schools, or make recommendations about renovations
- Businesspeople to run workshops for teachers on word processing, data bases, and spreadsheets
- Carpenters willing to build cabinets, bookshelves, and other items for classrooms or offices
- Doctors, nurses, and other health professionals to teach CPR classes, enliven biology and health classes, and advise about student health programs
- Experts in energy efficiency to study school buildings and recommend ways to save energy
- Librarians to give advice about enriching or modernizing school libraries
- Performers and speakers to provide assembly programs
- Public relations professionals to help the district increase public awareness about the schools, their accomplishments, and their needs
- Writers to help the district secure grants from government agencies

If you like the idea, the first step is to decide just whom you want to compile the directory for: one school, all the schools in a district, or maybe even all the schools in the county. In general, the skills directory will be so helpful that it's a shame to restrict its use, so think in terms of working with all the schools in, say, a ten-mile radius. Next, contact the superintendent's office in the school district or districts you have chosen to ask whether such a resource already exists and whether teachers would be receptive. The idea is a new one, so chances are your call will be met with considerable enthusiasm. The administrator may endorse your plan on the spot, but is more likely to want to confer with teachers before giving you the go-ahead.

When you get the district's agreement, there are a number of ways for you to solicit names for inclusion in the book. You can put notices in local newspapers, contact senior citizen centers, post flyers and leave sign-up forms at libraries and other key locations, contact churches and synagogues, send notices home with students, and make announcements at meetings of various kinds.

But the key to assembling a useful skills directory is that old standby, networking. If you undertake the activity as part of the work of a social club, a business group, a parents organization (see pages 53-55), or a local education foundation (see pages 90-110), the core of your network will be the members of the organization. If such organizations aren't available or aren't interested, recruit friends and neighbors and call a meeting to start compiling names. Think of everyone you know and what skill or knowledge they might be able to contribute. Then think of topics and see if the group can come up with names of people who might be knowledgeable in the field. Chances are that one meeting of your group will produce a list of 40 or 50 possible contacts.

But don't contact them yet. Build and refine your list over the next month or so. Have all of your core group make it a point to explain the project and get more suggestions everywhere they go — at work, while shopping, at parties. Then hold another meeting to add to the master list and prioritize contacts where there is more than one name in a category. If you've networked well, your list may now contain a hundred or more names.

The next step is to divide the names among members of the core group and begin active recruiting. Your conversation with the people you hope to list need not be long or complicated. Explain the concept of your skills directory and ask if they are willing to be included. Tell them that they are only committing to a few hours of their time, that school personnel will attempt to suit the volunteers' schedule, and that they are free to turn down a request if it is made at a bad time. And don't forget to talk about how good they'll feel sharing their talents with students and educators. Above all, be sure to ask those who seem interested if they know other people whose names should be in the book. You'll find that few of the people you call will turn you down and some will join your effort and do some networking of their own.

For all the people who agree to have their name in the book, gather all the information you will need to print: their name, phone number, address, and detailed information about how they are willing to help and what their qualifications are. This is the kind of data you will need to present in your guide:

SERVICE OFFERED: Willing to show high-quality videotapes of Mexican village and folk life, religious festivals, dances, etc.; can also bring Mexican clothing, art, jewelry, maps of regions discussed, and tapes of Mexican music; QUALIFICA- TIONS: Has traveled extensively in Mexico for over 20 years; speaks Spanish, though not fluently

SERVICE OFFERED: Willing to discuss Civil War battles, strategy, Lincoln, politics, diplomacy, role of African-Americans, domestic life of period; QUALIFICATIONS: Has master's degree in American history from Michigan State (thesis on Emanci- pation Proclamation); has taught Civil War at community college level; has visited all major battlefields

SERVICE OFFERED: Willing to spend up to ten hours training teachers in applications for Apple computers, assessing computers now in use at the school, advising re hardware/software purchases or re computer curriculum; QUALIFICATIONS: Avid user of Apples for over ten years; in charge of computer training for small company

You and your core group can decide when you have enough names to go to press. In a small town, 50 to 100 names will be a real contribution to the schools. In larger communities, you may want to wait until you can offer more. But don't be too anxious about making the book complete and perfect. It will always be a work-in-progress because people will be moving and changing jobs, and you will have new names to add. For that reason, the book itself should be inexpensively produced (probably computer printout that you have duplicated and put in a three-ring binder) and should state clearly that new editions or supplements will be published frequently, probably every year.

When you're preparing the guide for publication, take a small amount of time to make the book more useful to educators by including a simple index. It will probably be broken down into two broad categories: classroom assistance (with individual entries such as chemistry, Spain, Great Depression) and services (with entries such as carpentry, computers, and energy-saving).

Try to get media coverage when you present the book to the school. The publicity will reward people already included in the book and encourage others to sign on for future editions. The teachers will likely be thrilled to get their copies, but because the idea is a new one, they may forget to use it at first. Ask district administrators to encourage use of the book for the first month or two, until it becomes routine.

If the book proves successful, plan to revise it at least once a year. The easiest way to make changes is to mail the appropriate page to each person listed, with a request that he or she provide updated information and mail the page back to you. Of course, you will probably be adding new names too, which you will gather in the same way you compiled the original entries.

Start an "I Have A Dream" Project

Don't reject such tuition-guarantee programs as exclusively for the rich. It's true there are some millionaires involved in these programs, but so are many concerned citizens of far more modest means.

The concept was originated, or at least has been popularized, by Eugene M. Lang, a wealthy New York businessman. In 1981, Lang surprised his audience, and himself, with an impromptu commitment during his speech to 61 sixth-grade graduates of Public School 121 in Spanish Harlem. If they finished high school, he said, he would pay their way through college. He called his plan the I Have A Dream Project.

When Lang was told that between 60 and 75 percent of his "dreamers" would be likely to drop out before graduation, he began a program of sustained support for the students, arranging tutoring, taking them on special trips, and inviting them to his office for Saturday rap sessions. His key decision was to hire a full-time assistant to help the dreamers stay in school. The intervention worked; by early 1993, 45 of his 61 students had completed high school or gotten their General Education Development (GED) certificate and four more were working on getting their diploma or certificate. Of the high-school graduates, 34 had entered two-year or four-year colleges, and 5 had received bachelor's degrees from Bard, Barnard, and other colleges. Of those who finished high school, but chose not to attend college, almost all were gainfully employed.

Of course, some of Lang's sixth graders didn't make it. Some moved and lost contact with the program; one girl became a drug addict and lost touch with the group; and one boy spent time in jail for robbery and drug distribution. But Lang's disappointment about the few is more than balanced by his pride in the majority, both those who attended prestigious colleges and those who weren't interested in college but are more successful than they would have been without his help.

As important as Lang's help has been to his Harlem students, the major impact of his offer may be the inspiration it provided to scores of other sponsors to adopt classes of their own all across America. Today, there are 156 I Have A Dream projects, sponsoring over

10,000 students in 27 states, with 11 more projects in formation. Hundreds of similar projects, inspired by Lang's model, are working with tens of thousands of additional students throughout the country: the RAISE program in Baltimore, the Taylor Plan in Louisiana, the READY Program in New Jersey, the HOPE Program in Hawaii, the Children's Crusade in Rhode Island, and many more.

Your personal finances may not allow you to fund a class, but you can still act as a sponsor and seek funding elsewhere in the community. Or, if you can't make the ten-year sponsorship commitment, there are other roles you can play:

- You can contribute part of the money, so that someone else can be a sponsor. Some projects are funded by twenty or more benefactors who pledge $2,500 or $5,000 a year for six years.

- You can attempt to recruit others to become sponsors, funders, or facilitators of a project. The "others" can be wealthy individuals, foundations, or corporations. Several colleges have coordinated the formation of projects: Grinnell in Des Moines, Stanford in East Palo Alto, Yale in New Haven. Churches and synagogues have played major roles in starting projects in New York, Dallas, Chicago, Portland, OR, and other cities.

- Or you can volunteer your time to help a project coordinator guide a class of "dreamers" to high-school graduation.

If you'd like to help financially, you should know how much money we are talking about. The I Have A Dream Foundation says that, for classes adopted at the sixth-grade level, it costs an average of $350,000 to cover six years of programming and tuition support for 40 to 75 students (for an estimated annual budget, see Appendix F). Because Foundation policy now calls for adoption no later than at the fourth-grade level, costs are projected at $430,000. If the program is initiated earlier than the fourth grade, an additional $40,000 is required for each additional year students will be in the program.

But as Eugene Lang discovered, money is only a small part of the story, because poorly educated and poorly supported children are not likely to finish high school and be in a position to take advantage of an offer of funds. The only way an I Have A Dream project can succeed is through time-consuming intervention throughout the children's schooling. The I Have A Dream Foundation requires hiring a project coordinator whose job is to ride herd on the students and make sure they progress to graduation. Project coordinators are a combination of counselor, truant officer, cultural impresario, and education advocate. They monitor academic performance, arrange for tutoring, counseling, and social services, befriend family members, intercede with school and other authorities, and take students on trips to basketball games, plays, and college campuses. Project coordinators depend on an array of volunteers to help get dreamers to graduation: to tutor them, mentor them, plan enrichment experiences, find them summer jobs, take them on trips.

Helping to start an I Have A Dream project can be immensely time-consuming and immensely rewarding. Whether you want to personally sponsor or co-sponsor a class of dreamers, help fund a sponsorship, or volunteer your time to support a project near your home, the I Have A Dream Foundation (see Resources section) can provide you with expert advice and sympathetic support. The Foundation can also furnish limited information on other models of tuition-guarantee projects.

Start a School Partnership

Traditionally, American businesses, churches, and clubs have had no particular interest in, and no formal relationship with, their local public schools. But those days are over. Today, there are hundreds of thousands of school partnerships all across America. If your company, church, synagogue, labor union, college, club, governmental body, cultural institution, social service organization, or senior citizen group isn't involved yet, you can be instrumental in getting it to consider the idea.

School partnerships take many forms. They may involve giant corporations, "mom-and-pop" businesses, a church, a police department, a club, or virtually any organization interested in improving education. They may support one school or many, may have a single, narrow purpose or a broad agenda, may seek to support traditional programs or systemic reform. Ten years ago, many were known as adopt-a-school programs, but the term has fallen out of fashion because it suggests a weak, struggling school dealing with a strong, parental company or organization. Today, the strongest partnerships bring together several or many businesses and community groups to help schools achieve major goals.

Even a small school partnership can provide real benefits to schools, supporting public education in almost all the ways this book suggests for individuals, but bigger and better. An individual can vote; your church or union can encourage all its members to vote. An individual can become a mentor to a potential dropout; your club or college can provide fifty mentors. An individual can donate a used computer; your company or hospital can give the school ten computers when you upgrade to new models.

And then your company or community organization can do so much that an individual cannot. It can give tours of its facilities; advise schools about how to prepare students for the working world; provide managerial assistance to administrators; hire students or teachers as summer interns; provide a new local education foundation with an office or supplies; or donate products and services to support teachers.

In turn, schools, especially middle and high schools, can often benefit their partners. They can let cooperating organizations use their sports facilities, provide partners' employees with training to improve their writing or computer skills, or arrange shows of student art in bank lobbies or hospital halls.

Businesses may be the most likely partners for schools because they have much to give and much to gain. They, more than other organizations, are positioned to give managerial advice, volunteer time, used furniture and equipment, specialized knowledge about certain school subjects, internships for teachers and students, and a host of other services. They gain indirectly as schools produce better-educated workers and directly through tax breaks and good publicity. Consider these win-win situations:

> When ABC Company buys new desks, it donates the old ones to a school, takes a charitable gift deduction in the amount of their fair market value, and wins fans among the teachers who receive them and the public who reads about the gift in the newspaper.

> LMN Company offers to let the local education foundation use two empty offices, takes a deduction in the amount of their fair market rent, and wins the good will of the organization and of the community at large.

> The XYZ Restaurant replaces slightly worn carpeting in its banquet room and gives the old carpeting to three elementary schools. The restaurant takes a small tax deduction and wins friends among hundreds of local families.

Other community groups can also form partnerships that are vital to public education and beneficial to the partner:

> **Colleges and universities** are natural partners for pre-collegiate educational institutions. They can provide in-service training for teachers; help revise curricula; provide academic opportunities for top students; organize alliances of college and K-12 teachers in various disciplines; encourage teachers to attend on-campus lectures and conferences; encourage college faculty and students to become tutors and mentors for K-12 students; provide recognition for outstanding teachers and administrators; provide summertime research opportunities for teachers; provide facilities for art, music, and dance festivals; sponsor "Academic Decathlons" or other contests; hire high-school teachers as assistants in academic departments during summers and sabbatical

leaves; encourage minority and female students to pursue careers in math, science, medicine, and engineering; and encourage the hiring of high-school students as research assistants.

Cultural institutions can provide similar assistance within their areas of interest: art, science, technology, history, music, dance, theatre. Public libraries can offer special reading or lecture programs for teachers or students; conduct book fairs for children; begin a program to encourage parents to read to their children; help improve school libraries; promote exchange of information with school libraries to avoid purchasing duplicate materials; and strengthen collections of videos and other materials that teachers can use in the classroom.

Labor unions can advise schools about curriculum revision to meet changing needs of the workplace; help schools update their vocational/technical equipment; provide summer work and pre-apprenticeship activities for teachers and students; and arrange for visits to work sites.

Municipal governments can enter joint purchasing arrangements with schools; coordinate recreational activities; coordinate efforts to fight juvenile delinquency, vandalism, drug and alcohol use, teen pregnancy, and sexually transmitted diseases; share groundskeeping, recreational, audio-visual, and specialized computer equipment; share storage space; and provide such services as snow-removal and vehicle maintenance.

Senior citizen organizations can coordinate volunteer programs in which seniors participate in oral history projects, reading programs for young children, tutoring, mentoring, "foster grandparent" programs, and a variety of other activities.

Churches and synagogues can be valuable sources of volunteers. And while schools must avoid sectarian entanglement, they can take part in community advisory groups set up to help schools revise curricula in such areas as human relations, multiculturalism, values, family life and sexuality, and the history and beliefs of the world's religions. Religious groups can also coordinate their youth programs with school activities and assist boards of education in drafting policies concerning religious holidays, songs, symbols, and decorations.

Social service organizations — such as those concerned with drug and alcohol abuse, teen pregnancy, AIDS and other sexually transmitted diseases, psychological counseling, family counseling, and teen suicide — can coordinate their programs with schools and even establish satellite offices in school buildings.

An effective way for a small business or community group to increase the impact of its support for school reform is to join with others to coordinate and multiply efforts. Such coalitions can grow into major reform efforts; more than 1,000 businesses and other organizations in Dallas have formed a partnership with the city's 200 schools. Approaching a local or county chamber of commerce, some of which already have education committees, is a good way to begin building such an alliance, which might operate much like, or be part of, a local education foundation (see pages 90-110).

If your organization decides to get involved, you can get valuable assistance from the National Association of Partners in Education (NAPE). NAPE provides written materials and workshops on organizing or expanding school partnerships of all kinds (see Resources section).

Create a Local Education Foundation

One of the most effective ways for you to help public schools in your community is to help launch a local education foundation (LEF). A foundation sounds like a big deal, possibly only for the rich, but that's far from the case. There are well over a thousand LEFs in the country, in all kinds of communities, and many of them were established by average citizens looking for effective means of helping their schools.

Local education foundations are independent, community-based, tax-exempt, non-profit organizations dedicated to school improvement. They are long-lasting organizations that seek to rally the entire community to understand, value, and support its schools. They do not duplicate the programs or constituencies of other groups, such as PTAs, with their focus on parental involvement in individual schools. While most LEFs serve a single school district, they can also serve several districts or all the districts in a county or state.

LEFs generally aid schools by encouraging donations of money, donations of goods and services, volunteerism, and general community support. Of these, money is what school administrators and some LEF board members often have in mind as the chief goal, but the other outcomes are, in most cases, more likely and perhaps more beneficial to the long-term interests of the schools. Certainly, LEFs will never raise enough money to lower school taxes significantly and will probably founder if they are advertised as a way to replace lost public funds. Instead, the most successful LEFs typically seek to provide money (the sort that businesspeople would call "research and development funds"), volunteer help, and community support for new school programs that may become part of the regular budget if they succeed. When an LEF gives money, it will typically confer with district administrators, select a project, seek funds to support it and, when fundraising is complete, pass along the money to the district as a restricted gift (that is, a gift restricted to the purpose designated by the donor). A few wealthy LEFs are able to build endowment funds and use the interest they generate to pay for programs in behalf of schools.

At their best, LEFs become independent voices of their communities, capable of celebrating school successes, focusing attention on shortcomings and, in cooperation with school administrators, seek-ing solutions and reforms. They often have the ability to see schools and their needs in ways that school board members and school personnel, immersed in day-to-day events, cannot. Thus, they are able to assume the important roles of convener and broker, conven-ing members of the community to discuss issues relating to educa-tion and brokering community assistance to the schools. They may also be instrumental in bringing educators and community leaders together to lobby governmental units on behalf of local schools or to form coalitions to attack problems that go beyond school walls.

Just about the only criticism of LEFs is that they are most likely to achieve success in suburban communities that are already favored by high tax ratables and generous corporations. Thus, they may have a tendency to increase the resource gap between rich and poor school districts. The LEF serving the Beverly Hills Unified School District in California, for example, provides the schools with about $350,000 in extra funding each year, while many poor districts nearby get no such assistance.

LEFs are separately incorporated and have no formal relationship with boards of education. But that doesn't mean LEFs can ignore school boards. Boards of education generally have to approve any form of assistance offered to their schools, so they have the last word about support an LEF may wish to provide. Generally speaking, the most successful LEFs are those that have good working relationships with school boards.

A typical structure for an LEF is to have a board of directors of 15-25 citizens, with the school district superintendent or a designee as a non-voting, *ex officio* member. The superintendent then acts as a liaison between the two organizations, informing the LEF board about the goals and needs of the schools and keeping the school board abreast of the LEF's plans and concerns.

You think your community is too small, too poor, or too spread-out to support an LEF? There are successful LEFs in all these sorts of communities, though each set of circumstances generates a different type of LEF activity. In a small town, an LEF may never acquire large amounts of money or goods, but it may tap new sources of people power: volunteerism, interest in school reform, and participation in school elections, school committees, and other activities. A poor city may be an excellent candidate for an LEF that can act as a catalyst, convincing a wide range of community interests — businesses, municipal government, social service agencies, churches, and clubs — to unite in support of schools. It may also be able to attract some financial support from suburban corporations or foundations that feel an obligation to assist urban areas. A spread-out rural district may benefit from an LEF just because it is so diffuse. The LEF can serve to bring far-flung interests together in support of common goals.

It will be easier to establish a successful LEF for your schools if your community possesses:

Corporate headquarters. Nearby corporations are probably already involved in helping your school district and will welcome the LEF as an ally. Regardless of their current involvement, they are likely to be excellent sources of LEF board members, school volunteers, and donations of money and goods. Their primary interest will be in the communities where their facilities are situated and those where their employees live.

Small high-tech businesses. High-tech companies tend to be acutely conscious of the huge potential for use of technology in the schools and concerned about the need for improvements in math and science curriculum. They can be valuable sources of volunteers, expert advice, used equipment, and money.

A number of small thriving businesses. Small business owners are often keen supporters of community efforts to help schools produce the kinds of graduates they hire. Because they usually have strong ties to the local community, they are good sources of support for programs that can give them "good press."

Real estate development activity. Developers and realtors understand that good schools boost real estate values. They also know that major new residential developments may mean additional strains on the school system. For both reasons, they are often eager to help schools, sometimes with major donations of money, facilities, or land.

A long-established and well-reputed high school. Such a school has deep roots in the community. That means thousands of citizens who feel positively about the schools and may be willing to help the LEF accomplish its mission. It may also mean an opportunity to start a high-school alumni organization that will provide strong support for foundation programs.

A large community of retired professionals and other seniors. LEFs thrive on volunteers, and no volunteers are more desirable than skilled seniors looking for productive and satisfying ways to spend their time.

But the real key to success is something that is randomly scattered throughout the country, in rich districts and poor, in urban districts and rural: dedicated citizens. Without them, an LEF in the most favorable circumstances is bound to fail; with them, an LEF in the least favorable setting is likely to succeed. Your community has at least one such citizen. How else to explain why you're reading this book?

Steps in Forming an LEF

Who takes the lead in forming an LEF? Often it is a superintendent or principal who has heard about successful organizations in other districts and wants to spark interest in the local community. The administrator typically studies the topic thoroughly, gets preliminary approval from the board of education, perhaps including the authority to spend a modest sum on the effort, and then begins to network among community leaders to find potential supporters. Other possible initiators of LEFs are business executives representing one or more companies, chambers of commerce, and community foundations.

If you're not aware of any such activity in your community, your first step should be to arrange a meeting with administrators of the school or schools you would like to help. They may tell you that efforts to set up an LEF are already under way and refer you to those in charge. They may welcome you as an answer to their prayers. Or they may not know what you are talking about and be suspicious of the entire idea. In that case, it will be up to you to win their support and that of the school board; without such support, you will simply not be able to proceed.

Once the school administration agrees to cooperate, the experience of hundreds of LEFs provides a proven plan for you to follow in setting up your own organization:

Look for a champion. Your LEF is most likely to succeed if it is driven by a champion, someone who is convinced that the schools need community support, who is capable of spreading that conviction to others, and who is tireless in pursuit of his or her goals. Maybe you can convince the superintendent to be that champion. Maybe you are the champion. If not, you will have to network in your community until you find one. Consider the most active people in town. Consider the people that everyone looks up to and are proud to be associated with. Consider people who already know a good deal about education, perhaps a retired teacher or administrator. Avoid people who are identified with a single faction, whether it is a political party or a social group. And avoid people who might try to use the organization as a political instrument to oppose the school board.

Form a clear understanding with the school board and administrators. Initial misconceptions can grow into major impediments to LEF success. All parties must understand what the LEF hopes to do, what sorts of people will be asked to serve on its board of directors, and what its relationship with the school board will be. As in any business matter, this information should be put in writing, in a letter to the superintendent.

Assemble a steering committee of interested citizens. Up to this point you may have been working on your own. It's time to try out your ideas on a small group of fellow citizens, perhaps as few as four or five and no more than ten or so, representing different parts of your community. Depending on the tone you want to set, you might hold the meeting in your house, at a school, or at a place of business. When you assemble the steering committee, recruit people who would be good members of the LEF board, but don't exclude excellent candidates just because you think they won't serve in that capacity. Their help will be useful even over the short run and you may be underestimating how attached they will become to the project. Your initial meeting should be devoted to describing LEFs and discussing how one would function in your community. The superintendent or a deputy should be present to make a brief presentation about the schools, attest to the support of the board and administration, and answer questions. The meeting should conclude with plans for additional discussions.

Network with other LEFs in your area. There probably are active LEFs in communities like yours elsewhere in your state and you will learn much by talking to their board members about their experiences. Your state department of education (see Appendix H) may be able to guide you to appropriate organizations, as may the Public Education Fund Network or the National Association for Partners in Education (see Resources section for information about both organizations).

Choose a name and draft a mission statement. During the second meeting of the steering committee, you should be able to reach consensus on the purpose of your LEF, including just which schools it seeks to benefit. That will allow you to choose a name and compose a short, clear mission statement (see examples of both in Appendices A and B).

Draft preliminary bylaws. Drafting bylaws, organizational policies about how the LEF will function, may seem daunting, but is actually quite simple, since all non-profit bylaws are similar. The best model for your organization will be the bylaws of another LEF (see Appendix C), but you may wish to review those of several non-profits before making decisions for your group. In framing your bylaws, you will have to decide:

> **Will your LEF be a membership organization?** Will the board of directors be the only "members" of your LEF or will you also have a general membership category, where people pay an annual fee in return for some benefit, as do members of museums, and enjoy some kind of decision-making authority? Most LEFs designate the board as their only members, but you can keep your options open by authorizing the board to create additional classes of members at a later date.

> **How many board members do you want?** There is no ideal number, though a board that is too large — say, over 25 — will probably be unwieldy. Set a broad range in the bylaws; the lower number should be at least five, but low enough so you can recruit the necessary members quickly. The upper

figure should be the highest number you think can operate efficiently; you will probably not reach the full complement for several years. By no means should you fill all your board seats in the formative stage of your LEF, because you will almost certainly come upon wonderful candidates as you continue to network in the community.

What will be the terms, methods of election, and qualifications of board members? Three-year terms are common, but they should be staggered so that one-third of the board is elected each year. This can be done by simply drawing numbers to determine which board members will serve terms of one, two, and three years. Qualifications are usually expressed as exclusions; many LEFs exclude board of education members and employees from their boards. The same section of the bylaws will also name the superintendent or principal as a non-voting, *ex officio* member of the board. Avoid formal designation of seats on the board for various areas, interests, or organizations. Diversity can be achieved much more simply by choosing a wide variety of board members to fill the seats.

How frequently will you meet? Don't worry about making an accurate prediction; it's far too early to tell. Instead, indicate that the board will meet at least quarterly. You must designate a month for an official annual meeting, which you will probably want to be the first or last month of your fiscal year.

What will your fiscal year be? This is entirely up to you. The two most common for LEFs are the calendar year and the same fiscal year used by the school district (probably July through June).

What will be your quorum size? A quorum of one-half of the board plus one is common.

What officers will you have and how long will they serve? The classic configuration of president, vice-president, secretary, and treasurer is sufficient for most LEFs (typical duties of officers are presented in the sample bylaws in Appendix C). Some organizations create additional, ceremonial vice-presidencies to honor active or promising members, but this same effect can be achieved more directly. Officers are generally elected for one-year terms. Some organizations limit the number of consecutive terms for officers, or perhaps just for the president.

What committees will you have? Your LEF will need standing committees in charge of finance, fundraising, nominations, programs, and public information (typical tasks of these committees are spelled out in the sample bylaws in Appendix C). The bylaws should also permit the board to create additional committees, as needed.

Most steering committees can settle all these issues in a single meeting, with the understanding that bylaws can be amended if they turn out to be deficient in some way. Your bylaws must also contain several specific provisions in order to meet IRS requirements for recognition as a non-profit. An attorney should make sure the document includes these, and any provisions required by your state, before it is adopted at your first board meeting.

Select initial board members. This is one of the most critical steps in forming your LEF, because the group's success is likely to depend almost totally on the character and energy of its leaders. If your steering group is big enough (that is, as large as the minimum number of directors stipulated in your bylaws) and representative of at least several different parts of the community, its members can be the entire board. If you need to recruit more members at this point, do some brainstorming to generate additional names and then prioritize your list. Look for good communicators, corporate employees, small business owners, employers of your schools' graduates, labor leaders, religious leaders, members of organizations serving youth, people with strong commitments to public education, people with fundraising experience, and people from segments of the community not yet represented. Avoid politicians, recent members of the school board, and people who may be planning to run for the school board or other elective office. Try to include an attorney, an accountant, and a public relations professional, whose expertise will be valuable to the organization. When you have selected your targets and are ready to recruit them, have the steering committee member who knows the person best invite him or her to lunch, perhaps with a school administrator. When recruiting new members, be honest about time requirements and the expectation that they will donate to, and help raise money for, the organization.

Hold the first formal meeting of the board. After making sure that newly recruited members are comfortable with their role, launch the LEF by ratifying bylaws and nominating and electing officers. Then complete the formalities by asking an attorney to draw up incorporation papers and to submit an "Application for Recognition of Exemption" under Section 501(c)(3) of the Internal Revenue Code. The IRS letter confirming your 501(c)(3) status, which may take four to six months to process, will mean that gifts to your organization provide the donor with favorable tax treatment (many corporations and foundations will not consider requests for funds unless they are accompanied by a copy of the IRS letter). If there is no attorney among your board members, ask a local law firm to do the work as a contribution to the organization.

Form committees. To run efficient, productive board meetings, your LEF will rely on its committees to do the preparatory work. At your first board meeting, or soon thereafter, members should indicate their preferences for committee assignments, and the president should designate committee members. Until additional board members are recruited, committees will be very small and board members will have to serve on more than one. Their work load can be reduced if the board is willing to admit non-board members to committee deliberations, including, perhaps, some of the people who declined invitations to serve on the board itself. The board should charge its committees with initial tasks and suggest deadlines for completion. The program committee should be charged to recommend initial programs, the fundraising committee to study and present plans for raising money, and the public relations committee to make recommendations about announcing the LEF's formation, creating a brochure (see sample in Appendix E), and keeping its name before the public.

Open formal relations with the board of education. You should now inform the school board that the LEF has become a reality. The superintendent can tell you if it would be more appropriate to make a presentation at a board meeting or to write to the board. In either case, include a written description of your mission and your understanding of how the LEF will operate. Just to make sure you don't ruffle any feathers, it would be prudent to include a specific statement acknowledging the school board's responsibility for overseeing the operation of the schools, including its right to reject forms of assistance that the LEF might offer. At this point, the school administration may wish to respond by sending the LEF a letter of understanding about the relationship between the two organizations, and by asking the school board to adopt a formal policy on the subject.

Form an advisory committee. An advisory committee can be a great asset to a new LEF. A well-chosen one would include various experts, including teachers, who can provide advice, represent additional segments of the community, help raise funds, and move up to membership on the board. An advisory committee can also include well-regarded people who don't have time to work on behalf of the LEF, but who are willing to lend their names to help it gain recognition in the community.

Establish an LEF office. Your LEF needs a place to meet, a place to keep its files, and a place to receive mail and telephone calls. By no means does this imply that the organization should rent office facilities. At first, the board secretary's home can provide file space and a phone number (the officer's home number, until such time as phone traffic becomes too great); a post office box can serve as the mailing address; and the board and its committees can meet in public buildings, such as libraries, or in conference rooms of local businesses. During its first few months of existence, the LEF can seek donated office space by inquiring among corporations, colleges, community foundations, and chambers of commerce. Often, the school district itself may offer facilities and minor in-kind help, such as supplies, duplicating services, and secretarial assistance. The LEF can accept such assistance while it seeks more permanent arrangements, but should avoid giving the appearance to the community — and the IRS — that it is a mere tool of the school district.

Consider staff requirements. In an active LEF, a small board of directors will soon become burned out if it tries to manage programs in addition to carrying out board functions. Some LEFs have collapsed in their first few months of existence simply because board members weren't provided necessary support. On the other hand, an LEF should put off hiring staff for as long as it can, because salary money is difficult to raise, and funds are better spent for programs. The same thing is true of consultant services, though some school districts appropriate an amount sufficient to hire a consultant until the LEF is established, usually between $2,000 and $5,000. For most small LEFs, the solution is to recruit volunteers to perform staff functions. Ideally, a new LEF can locate a retired business or school manager to serve as unpaid executive director. For larger organizations and for small LEFs that have proved themselves, it may be possible and desirable to raise funds necessary to hire a part-time and, later, a full-time manager.

Whatever your role in establishing an LEF, try to keep it clear of problems that have crippled many promising organizations:

- Plunging into programs without getting firm agreement on the mission and goals of the organization
- Failing to clarify the roles of the school board and the LEF board
- Becoming identified with the school board in the public mind
- Allowing school administrators to dominate the LEF, limiting the role of its board members and depriving them of ownership of successes
- Recruiting top-flight board members, but burdening them with routine tasks such as drafting bylaws, filing incorporation papers, producing news releases, and writing letters
- Recruiting board members without being candid about their fundraising responsibilities

- Choosing board members who have hidden agendas, such as wanting to start a program to help their own children or running for the school board
- Allowing board members to influence decisions that involve, or appear to involve, conflicts of interest
- Trying to do too much too fast, usually by choosing an overly ambitious initial project

Initial LEF Projects

The two classic first projects for LEFs are publishing a skills directory, a list of local resources available to teachers and adminis-trators, and starting a mini-grant program for teachers. Both are relatively inexpensive, doable projects, are attractive to school personnel, provoke no controversy, build the morale of the LEF board, and provide opportunities for good public relations.

Skills directories are ideal first programs because they require very little cash outlay, and the networking necessary to compile them also serves to publicize the new organization throughout the community. Skills directories are discussed in full elsewhere, as a separate strategy (see page 78-82).

Mini-grant programs offer cash prizes to teachers who propose the most innovative or productive (or whatever attributes your LEF wants to encourage) class project. Larger districts may offer mini-grants to principals who propose low-cost, innovative programs for their schools. Funds needed are modest because many innovative projects can be accomplished very inexpensively; raising $5,000 will allow your LEF to award ten grants of $500 or five grants of $1,000. Grants for principals would probably be somewhat larger. These sums won't finance major changes, but they will permit all kinds of interesting projects that would otherwise be impossible. And the beauty of grant programs of any kind is that even educators whose proposals are rejected probably have done some innovative thinking and planning that will benefit their students outside of the intended project.

How will your LEF raise the necessary $5,000? Because the sum is modest, you might be tempted to fund the project with donations from your board of directors. There are two reasons you shouldn't do that. One is that some kinds of donations are easier to get than others. It is relatively easy to get money for interesting projects, but hard to get it for day-to-day operations. Save your director donations for less attractive expenditures and seek your mini-grant money elsewhere. The second reason is that by going to the community for mini-grant funding, you will be spreading understanding and support for your fledgling organization among business and other influential interests.

Local businesses are ideal targets for a mini-grant campaign because of the advertising value you can guarantee to donors. Tell them that if they donate enough for one or more of the mini-grant awards, you will give the grant in the name of their business and invite them to an award ceremony. There you will arrange for a heartwarming photograph of generous donor, innovative teacher, and adorable children to be sent to local media and framed for display at the donor's business. Who could resist such a pitch? Larger businesses might even wish to fund the entire grant program or commit to fund one or two named awards every year (for example, "the Annual Computer Depot Award for the Most Innovative Project Involving Computer Technology").

The Public Education Fund Network (see Resources section) has available an excellent packet of information on mini-grant programs, including timetables of activities and sample press releases, grant application forms, rejection letters, and award notices.

Later Projects

After your LEF scores a success with its first one or two projects, it will have gained the reputation and the self-confidence to seek bigger payoffs. The list of possibilities is endless and depends on the mission of your organization and the needs of your schools. A few suggestions will help you start thinking:

Start a high-school alumni society. This will only work if you are aiding a high school that has been in existence long enough to have a large number of graduates. Run by volunteers, such a society would organize reunions, publish a newsletter with stories about graduates and current school programs, seek donations, and sell school memorabilia. Appeals to alumni should stress restoration of programs that have disappeared since their graduation, physical improvements to the buildings they remember, and recognition of prominent faculty. An ideal program for an alumni association would be to seek funds — especially from doctors and scientists — to establish a "chair" for an influential science teacher of long standing or to establish a science award in his or her name. An auxiliary benefit of extensive contact with alumni is that it will undoubtedly establish links with institutions (colleges, corporations, foundations, associations, etc.) that may be able to aid the school district by way of cooperative programs, loans of personnel, loans of facilities, or gifts of equipment or money.

Start an academic decathlon project. If your LEF supports a number of schools, or if it can make arrangements with a county-wide organization, it could sponsor a series of academic competitions to reward excellence and increase student motivation to excel. A decathlon project might be held over a weekend on a college campus and feature quiz shows modeled on *Jeopardy* or other popular television programs, contests to showcase critical thinking skills, and presentations of science, art, music, drama, dance, and writing projects.

Open a clearinghouse for surplus furniture, equipment, and supplies. LEFs supporting larger districts or multiple districts can perform a useful function by acquiring storage space and collecting surplus desks, chairs, filing cabinets, computers, supplies, and other items for distribution to schools as needed. You would be offering a useful service to companies, which could deliver all items to a single location, and you will be likely to acquire tens or hundreds of thousands of dollars worth of goods for the schools.

Establish a community-wide mentoring or tutoring program. Mentoring efforts by individuals and companies are discussed elsewhere in this book (see pages 61-65). Your LEF has the potential to rally community-wide support for such programs and to have a major impact on your schools. The LEF's role would be to seek necessary funds, recruit and train volunteers, administer the project, and evaluate the results.

Tap the potential of seniors to benefit the schools. Your community's senior citizens are a great reservoir of support for your schools. Your LEF could provide the necessary links to bring them into tutoring, mentoring, and other volunteer programs, and to institute such intergenerational activities as oral history projects, entertainment programs in senior citizen housing, and student production of newsletters or videos for seniors.

Open a gallery for student art. If your LEF is interested in promoting the visual arts, think big: open an art gallery for the display and sale of student painting, sculpture, photographs, and crafts. The LEF would rent space if necessary, but would hope to find donated space (for which the donor could claim a tax deduction equal to the fair market rent). Local artists or managers of arts-related businesses would select the items to be displayed. Students would be paid to manage and staff the gallery, and artists would be paid when their work sold, minus a percentage necessary to sustain the operation. If all this sounds too ambitious, you might test the viability of a gallery by presenting student art shows in local facilities. Some corporations have gallery space which you may be able to use for this purpose.

Begin a before- and after-school program. With the help of your LEF, your schools could open their doors at six in the morning and lock up at eight or ten at night. Taxpayers would continue to fund regular school programs during regular hours. But the LEF would provide supervised play and educational activities before and after school. If a school has excess capacity, services could also be provided during the school day. The program would be supported largely by fees charged to parents, supplemented by grants from community employers.

Fundraising

While fundraising may not be the most important activity of LEFs, it is certainly a vital one. Where does the money come from to fuel such wonderful program ideas and to pay the expenses of your LEF while you are carrying them out? Possible sources include the LEF board itself, residents of the community, small businesses, corporations, foundations, governmental agencies, special events, and product sales. Here are some considerations to help your board determine the mix that is best for your LEF:

The board itself. Don't even think about seeking funds from others until 100 percent of your board members have contributed. They can set their own level, of course, and some may give very little, but see that everyone gives something as a demonstration to potential funders that you are fully committed.

Residents of the community. These people will benefit from the programs of your LEF, so they are likely supporters of your efforts. One plan would be to send a letter to residents explaining the LEF's mission, seeking community input about needs and possible projects, and requesting donations. The success of such an appeal will depend largely on the affluence of your community and on current economic conditions. One wealthy New Jersey community landed $15,000 with its first letter of this kind and $25,000 from a second letter (admittedly during the booming mid-1980s). This sort of success can only be achieved by understanding the desires of the community and by holding out promise of satisfying them. In the New Jersey instance, parents concerned about declining programs for gifted students welcomed LEF plans to offer foreign languages and other enrichment courses after school and on Saturday. In less affluent communities, letters to residents will not produce such spectacular results and, until your LEF has proved itself with well-publicized successes, may actually antagonize some people. Your board is the best judge of the merits and timing of such an appeal.

Small businesses. Local companies are likely contributors to your LEF because their owners and employees live in your community and send their children to the schools you are trying to improve. The most helpful companies are likely to be those, such as real estate brokers, real estate development firms, and banks, with a stake in quality schools and those who number children among their customers or consumers. Small companies are more likely to help if you can offer them good publicity in return for their gift (see page 87).

Corporations. Don't fall into the common fantasy that corporations are swimming in money and will donate to your LEF as soon as it is formed. Most corporations will first want to see that you have a strong board, that your organization has already attracted support from the community, and that it has programs that offer a reasonable chance to solve specific problems. There are exceptions to this generalization. Some corporations will contribute a small amount in start-up funds to promising non-profits in their immediate vicinity and some will give an annual grant of $1,000-$2,000 to any organization whose board includes a corporate employee. Of course, anything is possible in the event that you have a personal connection to the corporation's top management or its director of giving. Where you lack such connections and the corporation is not in your backyard, you should try to fund some successful programs on your own before asking for corporate support. Corporations, like almost all funders, are more likely to look favorably on requests for program money than on appeals for less glamorous operating expenses. Corporations, like small businesses, are attracted by opportunities for favorable publicity, so the best request might be for an innovative program that the company can link its name with, or for equipment that will bear the name of the giver. For information on recent giving practices of local corporations and the names of key decision-makers, consult the latest edition of the annual *Corporate Giving Directory* in your library. The Taft Group, publisher of the *Directory*, also publishes the monthly *Corporate Giving Watch*, which contains the most recent information.

Foundations. Are there foundations in your community or your state that might provide your LEF with start-up or program funds? The way to find out is to consult the *Foundation Directory* and other publications of the non-profit Foundation Center. Your local city, state, or college library is likely to have a copy of the current *Directory* (it is published annually, and a supplemental volume updates it at mid-year), which will identify sites in your state with extensive collections of Foundation Center materials. But first, use the directory itself, either by scanning through the foundations in your state or by using its indexes.

Look for two kinds of foundations: those that are in your immediate vicinity and those that give grants to improve elementary and secondary education. For each entry, pay special attention to the section called "Limitations" to make sure that the foundation gives grants of the kind you seek to non-profits in your geographic area. In this way you can construct a list of the foundations most likely to support your LEF. The first approach should be a personal one if any of your board members know someone associated with the foundation. If not, the *Directory* will guide you about what sort of written proposal is appropriate. Appeals to foundations should set out clearly how much money you seek, the nature of your organization, the problem you seek to remedy, how you plan to address the problem, and how you will evaluate your success. The *Foundation Directory* and a number of books available in your library or bookstore can help you refine your research techniques and write winning grant proposals.

Governmental agencies. Government grants will not provide start-up or operational funds for your LEF and are not the most likely funders of your programs. Still, they may have potential under certain circumstances. The easiest way to review possibilities for federal funding is to consult the Education Funding Research Council's *Guide to Federal Funding for Education*, available in many libraries. In it, you will see that non-profits are eligible to apply for many federal grants. Your LEF, for example, might convene a consortium of non-profits to provide mechanisms for greater parent involvement in your district and apply for funding from the Family-School Partnership Program of the Fund for the Improvement and Reform of Schools and Teaching. Reading through descriptions of federal programs, in fact, may be a good way for your program committee to generate ideas for more ambitious projects.

Special events. Most special events are another way to attract local support for your LEF, but they do so in a less direct way than a letter to residents or a door-to-door appeal. Special events often take a lot of volunteer time and sometimes produce little revenue after costs are subtracted. But they have a secondary benefit in that they serve to publicize the organization and introduce its board and other supporters to a number of potential contributors. Examples of special events are a local dinner-dance, an annual house tour, periodic wine-tasting parties, concerts, and lectures. Special events have added appeal when they connect with or advance the mission of the LEF. One such example is an academic awards dinner, combining fundraising potential, public relations, and recognition of top students — and perhaps top teachers — in the schools.

Product sales. Depending on your community, you may be able to raise modest amounts of money and to publicize your LEF and its mission through the sale of products. Possible items to consider are mugs, T-shirts, and sweatshirts with messages boosting the schools or education in general, and bumper stickers bearing such messages as "Proud Parent of an Honor Student at Jefferson High." The obvious drawback is that you will have to confront such potentially time-consuming issues as accounting, inventory, and storage. And, of course, you may misjudge demand and lose money on some of your products.

Whatever the targets of your fundraising efforts, these principles will help your board accomplish its financial goals:

Have a fundraising plan before you begin fundraising. Your LEF cannot raise funds in a coherent way unless it first considers the organization's needs and the community's capacity to supply them. The LEF's fundraising committee and board of directors will need to engage in serious discussions to cost out programs and administrative operations, ensure that they are realistic in terms of the community's ability to sustain them, identify appropriate funding sources, and forge long- and short-range plans for contacting them.

Involvement precedes commitment; commitment precedes funding. If you plan to seek funding from nearby corporations or foundations, or from wealthy individuals, involve them in the planning and implementation of your LEF. If your organization begins to produce results, they will become committed; if they are committed, they will be far more likely to provide financial support.

Try to "ring the chimes" of potential funders. Your LEF's proposals to potential funders, especially foundations and corporations, should stress themes that funders like to see: uniqueness of your proposed program, likelihood that the program will become financially self-sufficient within a few years, and creation of new alliances to solve problems.

Public relations and fundraising go hand in hand. People cannot be expected to give money to organizations they know little about. That's why your LEF's public relations committee must be active in the organization's infancy. If the committee is successful, it will generate news stories about the founding of your LEF, appointment of new board members, announcement of programs, receipt of financial and other donations and, of course, successful results. Publicity about donations is doubly useful because, in addition to spreading the reputation of the LEF, it rewards the giver.

Say "thank you" often and as creatively as you can. Expressing thanks is far more than polite; it is one of the most effective ways to attract more giving. Benefactors should be thanked in writing, in newspaper articles, in LEF brochures, in school newsletters, and in every oral presentation. Fortunately, LEFs have opportunities to say thanks in very appealing ways. Whenever possible, donors should be sent a framed photograph of students benefiting from the donation. The aim is to get that photograph on the giver's wall, where he or she will see it every day.

Programs drive funding, but can be modified to increase their appeal. Successful non-profits do not find out what money is available and then invent a program to capture it; they plan promising programs and then seek funds from suitable donors. Still, there may be opportunities for your LEF to modify one of its programs slightly to be more attractive to particular funders. An LEF seeking funds to permit student broadcasts on a cable television local access channel, for example, might add plans to aim some programming at senior citizens in order to become eligible for funds from a foundation with such interests.

The most common reason for not giving is, "I was never asked." Somewhere in your community there may be a retired farmer capable of leaving the LEF $100,000 in his will, a CEO of a small high-tech company willing to fund innovative science education projects, or a graduate of your district who would feel a great sense of accomplishment if she could play a major role in starting a school theater program. But they will probably never give a dime unless someone from your board summons the courage and takes the time to ask them.

People give to people. Which non-profit would you be most likely to support? The one you see advertised on television? The one that sends you a letter asking for help? Or the one that sends a good friend of yours to ask for your assistance? The answer is obvious, and your LEF should employ person-to-person fundraising wherever possible. This means using the connections you already have and developing new ones. A hard-working board will constantly seek opportunities to befriend the people who make funding decisions for businesses and foundations, or their spouses, their brothers, their mothers, or their best friends. Much of fundraising is networking to make the right connections so that you can make a personal appeal.

Local education foundations offer one of the most promising avenues for citizens to unite in support of their public schools. The large amount of work they require has its payoff in the creation of an organization which will benefit students in your community for decades to come, perhaps in ways you never dreamed of. It's possible that an LEF won't work in your community. But there is very little to lose, and much to gain by making the attempt.

Join an Advocacy Group or Become a Citizen Advocate

Do you have a particular issue you want to see addressed by your schools? Are you concerned, for instance, with the access handicapped children have to an appropriate education? Or perhaps you feel that gifted and talented students are being shortchanged. Or that girls are being discriminated against in classrooms. Or that ability grouping is perpetuating racist stereotypes. Or that your school should place more emphasis on math and science. Or that administrators should devote more time to identifying and training ineffective teachers. Or that discipline and school safety precautions are too lax. Maybe you are just generally concerned with the quality of education the students in your district, region, or state are receiving. Whatever it is you would like to see changed, a good way of making it happen is by joining an advocacy group or by creating such a group.

Is there already an advocacy group for your favorite cause in your community? It may be difficult to find out, especially if the group is not very active — not picketing, not filing legal suits, not getting mentioned in newspaper articles. But if a group exists, you ought to be able to find it by doing a little networking. Call your district or school office, the parents organization (PTA, PTO, etc.), and your local reference librarian. Attend a few school board meetings and talk to other attendees. If these efforts don't produce any results, you can be pretty sure that the field is wide open and you can start your own group.

One Man's Story

If you start down this road, there's no telling where you'll end up, but your journey is likely to be fulfilling. Consider the case of Herb Green of Plainfield, New Jersey. Like many people, Green became involved with the public school system about the time his children entered school. At that time, the mid-1960s, Plainfield was under orders to eliminate its totally segregated school system — a system that clearly discriminated against black children. Black schools were so poorly maintained that you knew the color of the students inside by looking at the building's exterior. The education was inferior also. Teachers who were judged unsatisfactory in white schools were almost always transferred to those attended by blacks.

But integration didn't come easy. The racial division in the community was painful. Whites reacted to the inclusion of blacks in "their" schools by fleeing the district. As they left, they were replaced by minorities.

Green, who is white, wanted to make sure Plainfield's students got not only an integrated education, but a high quality one as well. And he wasn't quiet about it. Even before his sons entered school, he attended board of education meetings and, in his normally booming voice, spoke out about the desegregation plans. Integration must take place, he insisted to the foot-dragging board, but the level of education must also remain high. By becoming active in the PTAs of his sons' schools and, eventually, chairman of the district's PTA Presidents Council, Green rallied his troops. Together, at meeting after meeting and through every public means possible, they voiced their concern about the slow pace of integration, the lack of regard for quality education, and the political game-playing within the system. But the board and district administration refused to listen.

Eventually, Green noticed he was becoming a leader with fewer and fewer followers. As whites fled Plainfield, the city, with its beautiful old homes, had become attractive to middle-class blacks. Now, in the late 60s and early 70s, they, too, were leaving. Discouraged, they were moving out because the school district had transformed itself into a "remedial" district — one that aimed all its instruction at the poorest students. They could no longer get the education they wanted for their children. Green found there were fewer and fewer people speaking out for quality education.

Then the mayor, who had consistently said he would never appoint "that rabble-rouser" to the board of education, surprised everyone by changing his mind. Green used the opportunity to start a course for parents. Its purpose was to create a new cadre of people to push for quality, integrated education — a cadre made up of those who were left behind after the exodus of middle-class whites and blacks. Since school board meetings can be pretty intimidating if you don't understand the issues or the policies being considered or how the system works, Green's course provided them with those kinds of information.

This was the mid-70s, when New Jersey was embroiled in a law suit about school finance that eventually resulted in the imposition of an income tax — which was supposed to equalize school funding — and greater accountability for schools by way of minimum basic skills testing. The latter was fiercely opposed by teacher groups and others with a vested interest in the status quo. Arrayed against them were a mix of organizations ranging from the business community to a ministerial association. When a New Jersey foundation offered to provide start-up money to link these organizations in a state-wide citizen advocacy group, called Schoolwatch, Green left his career in the television industry to take on the role of full-time education advocate.

Under Green's direction, Schoolwatch became a constant presence in the state legislature, testifying on issues affecting the public schools. It also formed teams of parents to monitor county superintendents' offices, which were supposed to assess the quality of education in local schools. The teams were created to keep county officials "honest" and to minimize "old boy" connections which, where old friends were responsible, sometimes allowed school failure to go uncriticized. Some county superintendents welcomed these teams and even went so far as to include them in their monitoring visits to local schools. Others, however, treated them with suspicion and hostility.

The members of Schoolwatch shared Green's vision of training parents to be more effective in influencing the quality of education in their local districts. However, they knew Schoolwatch itself could not sponsor such a program — the group was too controversial. Like any effective advocacy group, they had irritated just about everybody at one time or another.

So they established a second organization — The Institute for Citizen Involvement in Education. Using a small grant from a foundation in North Carolina, Institute staff developed a curriculum covering such topics as school administration, discipline, testing, parent involvement, funding, and teacher contracts. Since 1981, various versions of the Public Policy and Public Schools course have been given numerous times in New Jersey, Chicago, and New York City. Sponsored by local school boards or by grants, the course provides free books and materials to participants.

The course has been a tremendous success, breeding hundreds of local advocates for quality education. In some districts, classes have stayed together to press for changes in their districts or to ask tough questions about the district's budget. In Plainfield, for instance, one class conducted a successful campaign to replace the appointed school board with an elected one. On another level, the course, by offering college credit to those who complete it, has encouraged many of its graduates to pursue college programs they otherwise might not have attempted.

In the mid-80s, Green went on to co-found a third organization, the Public Education Institute (PEI), which he currently heads. PEI now sponsors the Public Policy and Public Schools course (see Resources section) as well an on-going series of seminars on education and youth policy attended by educators, health and social service professionals, and other citizens from across New Jersey. While not an advocacy group per se, PEI has created a network of people who care about children and the education they receive, has called attention to issues in children's health as well as public education, and has planted seeds for change in the state. It has also sponsored programs that stimulate high-school students' interest in education issues and widen the horizons of mid-career professionals to greater opportunities for collaboration in improving the lives of young people.

How to Begin

You don't have to become a full-time school advocate to achieve some of Herb Green's successes. If there already is a group in your community, you're ahead of the game, but if there isn't, you can still be successful. Begin small, set reasonable goals, and work for what you believe in. And get others to join you. Numbers count. The more people and organizations you have espousing a particular issue, the more likely you are to get the bureaucracy to respond.

Never organized anything, you say? Sure you have. You've put together birthday parties, dinners for friends, club or church fundraising events, group picnics, business activities. The principles are the same. Organizing means:

- defining your mission;
- asking people to participate;
- reaching consensus;

- planning activities to meet specific goals;
- dividing up responsibilities; and
- following up.

The first thing you'll want to do is to form a core group — a small number of like-minded people who are willing to press for change. You can find them by advertising in your local newspapers, posting notices on bulletin boards, and talking with your friends. It doesn't matter if your friends aren't excited about your goals; they might know someone who is (see pages 37-40 and 93-101 for more ideas on organizing). Once your core group (it doesn't need to be more than three or four people) is in place, you can start the ball rolling.

What Advocates Can Do

Whether you have joined an existing group or have started your own, here are some things you might find yourself engaged in:

Organizing public meetings. Public meetings are a good way to bring together people who have some concern about or interest in an issue. They have two purposes: to alert people to the importance of your issue and to get additional members for your group.

If you decide to hold a public meeting, you will need to set a date — giving yourselves a month or two to advertise and get the word around — and to reserve a convenient meeting place. Perhaps your library or a local church will provide free or low-cost space. You will also have to decide on the format for your meeting. Do you want a single speaker or a panel? Perhaps a workshop format consisting of small groups considering various aspects of the issue would work better.

Try to come up with a catchy slogan to emphasize your issue. Use it on flyers and other advertising for your meeting. But don't depend on advertising alone to bring in attendees. Personally invite particular people, local clergy or business people, for instance — maybe even your congressman and state, county, and municipal representatives. Inform the news media as well.

At the meeting, ask for volunteers. Make a list of their names and telephone numbers and then follow up with phone calls inviting them to your next meeting or activity.

Conducting public information campaigns. Public information campaigns are a good way to educate the citizenry and to build interest in your issue. You might choose to conduct one early in your effort to bring about reform, so that others will be motivated to lend you their support.

Conducting an information campaign will be a whole lot easier if you have co-sponsors, especially if your group is still small. You might even get your school district to join you if they see the effort as informational rather than confrontational. The district might be happy to cooperate, for example, if you want to educate the community about inadequate science labs and equipment. The goal here is to get information out in as many ways and to as many people as possible. That means writing press releases, getting articles published in newspapers, plastering the community with posters, setting up information booths at shopping centers, getting speakers before local groups, and passing out flyers. Be sure to include on your flyers the names and phone numbers of one or more organizers, so that people can call for more information. Make a list of those who respond, and follow up with an invitation to join your group.

Organizing a march or a public rally. These kinds of activities are most appropriate just before a decision is to be made by an agency or governmental body. Perhaps your issue is to go before the board of education in a few days, or is about to be voted on in the state legislature. That's the time you'll want to demonstrate the strength of the force supporting your position on the issue.

Because strength is shown by the number of people marching or attending a rally, you will have more clout if you work with co-sponsors. The tasks you and your colleagues will have to undertake include advertising, lining up speakers, designating a spokesperson, assigning marshals to keep order, contacting the press, and getting signs and buttons made (use your catchy slogan).

Choose an appropriate site for your march or rally. If yours is a local issue, you might demonstrate around a school or in front of the district office. The state Capitol steps are often used for broader issues. You will need to make arrangements with public safety officials in all cases.

Conducting a mail campaign. This activity is most appropriate for times when you want to influence either state or national legislation. Attending and speaking out at municipal government or school board meetings is a more effective way to shape local ordinances and board policies.

Time your mail campaign to coincide with the key steps in the law-making process: when a bill is on a committee agenda; when it is due to be voted on by a house of the legislature; when it is being considered by a conference committee; and before it is signed into law.

To begin a mail campaign, reproduce a list of the legislators you want contacted. Distribute that list, along with information about the pending legislation, to your members and to others who support your goals, and urge them to write. Ask people to report back on responses they receive from legislators. Don't forget to send thank-you letters to legislators who support your position.

Testifying at public hearings. Thoughtful, well-organized, and concise presentations of your group's views at public hearings are an effective way of getting your message across to decision-makers. Hearings are held by local governments and school boards, state boards of education, and state and federal legislative committees.

Often you will be required to sign up in advance of the hearing in order to speak. Get the names of a number of your most articulate supporters on this list (with their permission, of course), help them put together their presentations, then round up your members to attend the hearing and lend moral support to the speakers.

Holding press conferences. Press conferences are a good way to get publicity for your views. But be aware that with the news media (press, television, and radio) timing is everything. If you hold your conference immediately after bad news has been announced or when your group is about to issue a potentially controversial report, you are more likely to get their attention than on "less newsworthy" occasions. Also, understand that reports of your conference might be buried at the back of the paper or ignored altogether if something more exciting comes along.

Begin organizing the press conference by sending a press release to all the newspapers, television and radio stations you want to invite, with information regarding the date, time, place, and purpose of the conference. Daily newspapers have editors for various sections of the paper and reporters assigned to cover specific topics (state government, for instance, and sometimes education) and different geographical regions, so you should telephone these

newspapers to determine the proper persons to receive the information. Weeklies often have just one editor and only one or two
reporters, so getting the information to the right person is less of an
issue. Call the news departments of television and radio stations for
the names of those you should contact. Again, the difficulty in
finding the right person will depend on how big the news staff is
and how many hats each individual has to wear.

Plan to hold the press conference at a convenient or symbolic
location, such as the lobby of the school district offices or outside
the state Capitol. Hold it in the morning, if possible, so there is
plenty of time for your story to make the evening television news
and the next edition of the paper. Before 9 a.m. of the day of the
conference, call the editors of all invited papers and the news
departments of TV and radio stations to confirm their attendance.
At the conference, hand out a prepared statement, have a spokesperson present the issue and your group's response to it, and answer
all questions.

Advice

After almost thirty years as a school advocate, Herb Green says
he still believes real change takes place on the local level. State and
national groups need to make an effort to provide resources and
support to local people, he says. To those who are working for
improvement of their local schools, he has this advice:

- Don't assume everybody is your enemy. Look for the
  school board member or the teacher who shares your
  views, and enlist their aid;

- Don't think you need agreement on every issue — find the
  common ground and work on that;

- Look to PTAs and other parent organizations; contact
  businesses, heads of youth service agencies, the police,
  hospitals and the medical community, welfare agencies,
  YM/YWCAs, etc., and form a joint task force; then bring
  in the schools — collaboration is important;

- Ask what might be possible, look for allies, and do it.

Here is some additional advice:

- Make a distinction between bureaucrats and public servants. A bureaucrat is the person who says things like: "It's not my job — go see the guy down the hall." "I'm sorry, but there's nothing I can do." "We don't have the money." "We're doing the best we can." "We're the professionals here." "You have to follow the proper procedures." The bureaucrat will not rock the boat; the public servant will do whatever he or she can to make things right for kids.

- Research the problem — know what you're talking about and don't allow yourself to be intimidated by someone with a know-it-all air. Be prepared to support your position with documents.

- Understand your opposition — what motivates them and what might be keeping them from doing what you feel needs to be done.

- Don't accept excuses from those who have the power to change things. Be persistent and don't let the buck get passed.

- Offer solutions, don't just talk about problems.

- Keep a sense of humor and don't lose your cool.

- Learn when and when not to compromise.

- Write things down and date your notes — summarize meetings and agreements, and distribute them to participants.

- Never threaten something unless you are able and willing to carry it out.

- Make sure your goals are clear. If you don't know what you are trying to accomplish, neither will your potential supporters, and no one will ever know if you are making progress.

- Use multiple strategies to achieve your goals.

- Gain the support of your community — involve as many people as you can in your efforts.

- Don't lose sight of your goal.

Hurdles

Advocacy groups are hard to sustain. When you are depending on volunteers to do the work, you will find it difficult to get the same people together consistently. Also, issues are often complex, and people tend to lose interest when a group goes round and round in its discussions. When you are working at the state level, it is even more difficult. "It's hard to keep an advocacy group going in a diverse community," says Herb Green. "It inevitably turns to questions of race and class." Urban issues are not supported by suburban groups. Suburban issues seem irrelevant to urban groups. Also, can whites speak for blacks? Can blacks speak for Hispanics? "It's hard now to get people to unite to advocate for all kids," said Green.

It is important to keep your group going, even after you achieve your initial goals. If your group succeeded, let's say, in instigating improvements in your district's special education program and then disbanded, what would happen if the board decided to withdraw most of the program's funds? A dead group can't respond to the next crisis or prevent it from occurring. Here are some things you can do to sustain the life of your advocacy effort:

- Refocus the group and tackle a problem you haven't had time for;

- Continue to monitor the activities of state and local bureaucracies — you never know when something critical may be brewing;

- Continue to hold regular meetings — the ongoing contact is important to group cohesiveness;

- Look for new talent to bring into the group — people who will stimulate others in new ways;

- Remain open and democratic and avoid becoming cliquish — people will drop away if they sense there is an "in-group." Look for ways to keep all your members involved; and

- Continue to communicate regularly with all your members, through personal and written contact, such as a regular newsletter.

Rewards

Accomplishing your goals is, of course, the biggest reward you can expect for your efforts. But sometimes you'll find more ordinary things rewarding. "You know," said Herb Green, "it may sound trivial, but I get real pleasure every time I look at the doorbell beside the front door of Plainfield High School. It used to be that whenever I or anyone else wanted to attend a board meeting, we had to pound on the door and shout to be admitted. I had to fight to get that bell installed, so whenever I use it, I smile."

You may also find, like other education advocates, that your influence has been felt far beyond your original intentions. Herb Green's greatest satisfaction comes from knowing hundreds of people across the state and the nation who speak up for the needs of children; he probably wouldn't admit it, but his efforts have been an inspiration to many of them.

Volunteer As a Citizen Advisor to Your State Legislator

If you would rather devote your energy to changing state policy than to working directly with schools or children, consider becoming an education advisor to a state legislator. You don't have the credentials to be an advisor, you say? Don't be too sure.

State legislators are desperately in need of assistance in dealing with the complicated matters they are asked to vote on: waste disposal, health care, mass transit, corporate taxes. Many legislators know very little about public education, one of the largest line items in the state budget. They may manage to get some advice from their staff and from biased "experts" employed by special interest groups. But they probably do not have anyone they can rely on to study education issues and provide them with balanced advice, particularly about the local impact of proposed legislation. It doesn't take a doctoral degree and decades of experience in schools to provide that kind of help.

What it does take is time, dedication, and integrity. As an education advisor to a legislator, you will have to provide quick reports on bills and other materials sent to you for review; legislators often get little advance notice of upcoming action. You will have to avoid letting your private prejudices taint your advice. And you will have to keep informed about education in general and about the pros and cons of specific issues.

If the idea interests you, write or call legislators who serve your community and surrounding areas. You may need to talk to an aide first, but make it clear that you're offering free assistance and they will at least give you a hearing. If current legislators aren't interested, consider getting in on the ground floor by offering your services to a legislative candidate during the next election campaign.

To advise properly, you will need to develop a system for getting general and specific information about education issues. For general information, it's hard to beat *Education Week*, a tabloid-size newspaper containing essential news and features about pre-college education. On specific issues, ask to be put on mailing lists of three organizations in your state, all of which are active in trying to influence legislation: the state school boards association, the state school administrators association, and the state teachers association or associations (affiliates of the National Education Association and/or the American Federation of Teachers). As you can see, these groups represent the interests of the key players in public education. All three go through their own process of analyzing and issuing position papers on legislative bills. If you tell them that you are an education advisor to Assemblyman Jones, they should be eager to have you read their periodicals and position papers. All three organizations should have offices in your state capital; if your telephone company can't provide phone numbers, ask your state department of education for assistance in locating them.

Another prime source of information will be personal contact with educators, reformers, and average citizens. You should, of course, see schools in session and attend at least a few board of education meetings. If you are able, attend meetings of the education committees of both houses of your legislature. They generally hear testimony from all sides of an issue, which will make you better able to reach your conclusions and provide good advice. Committee meetings are also a great place to meet representatives of groups you may want to cooperate with.

A Case History

Here's how the process developed for Carl Sanderson (a fictional composite of several advisors). Carl retired a few years ago from a middle-management position with a large corporation. He had always been interested in education, especially while his daughters were in school, and had served one term as a school board member. Later, he had served on advisory committees, one studying the high-school science curriculum and one forming recommendations about multiculturalism. He hadn't been active in the past five years, but had read articles and books about America's schools and was convinced that the future of the country depended on its ability to improve its system of public education.

When he retired, Carl devoted about two days a week to consulting work and decided to devote another two days to the cause he had come to believe was so important to the nation. He considered volunteering as a tutor or mentor to a potential dropout, but wanted to have an effect on more than one or two students. He considered running for his local school board again, but remembered how restricted it was by state regulation. He decided to exert his influence on policy at the state level.

Carl called the three state legislators who represented his district, phoning them at their local offices rather than at the state Capitol. One professed not to need assistance (from his voting record, Carl suspected that he blindly followed the advice of the state teachers organization); the second never returned Carl's calls; but the third expressed great interest and asked Carl to lunch.

Elected only six months before, Assemblyman Wilson confessed to Carl that he was completely swamped by his legislative responsibilities. He was especially concerned about education bills; over 300 had been introduced that year. He knew that some were vitally important, but didn't have the time or knowledge to study them properly before casting his vote. His concerns were both moral — he felt it was unethical to vote for things he didn't fully understand — and practical — sooner or later, one of his votes was going to hurt the interests of his constituents and his legislative career would be over. Moreover, Wilson had co-sponsored a few education bills that he didn't completely understand. Now he was being asked about modifications to one of them and he didn't know enough to avoid embarrassing himself.

Carl spelled out his background and his thoughts about education reform. He assured Wilson that he was not an advocate for any education pressure group or association, and that he had his private biases, but could keep them under control. Then he offered Wilson a deal. Carl would devote two days a week to reading bills and background materials, including position papers of all the relevant interest groups. He would write memos to Wilson, summarizing what he had read and suggesting a course of action. His first priority would be education bills that were moving through the committee process and due to come to the floor for a vote. When he caught up with proposed legislation, he would talk to school personnel, school board members, and concerned citizens in the legislative district to discuss their concerns and what bills Assemblyman Wilson might introduce or support to address them. In return, all Carl asked was that the legislator read and provide feedback about his memos. Wilson readily agreed.

The relationship worked well. Wilson was delighted with Carl's first few memos and came to rely on Carl's assessment and advice. In studying the backgrounds of bills, Carl read widely and became much better informed about a wide array of education issues. When Carl began to talk to local educators, he uncovered a problem with transportation funding that could be alleviated by state action and actually drafted legislation that Wilson introduced, argued for, and got passed.

When Wilson was re-elected, he was appointed to the education committee. At Carl's suggestion, he began reading books and articles about school reform and became outspoken in support of school-site management (see page 149-150). With Wilson's increased role in education, Carl recently began to devote three days a week to his volunteer role. Today, Carl jokes that he's working harder now than before he retired, but he expresses a great sense of fulfillment. He is now playing a real role in the formation of state education policy.

Become a School Aide

Do you enjoy working with children? Are you looking to do more than volunteer work? You could become a teacher, but if that requires more time than you have available or more education than you have or want to get, perhaps you could take a job as a school aide.

School districts hire aides for various purposes. Classroom aides are used in elementary and, sometimes, in middle schools (grades 6-8) to increase the ratio of adults to students and to give students more individual attention. City schools, which often have large class sizes, frequently use aides for this purpose. Since these school systems are often under severe budget constraints, they find it is more economical to hire aides than to add teachers and build classrooms. More affluent districts sometimes use aides for the same reason, but crowded classrooms in these districts are more likely to be the result of rapid rises in student enrollment and are relieved as soon as new schools are built. More often, affluent schools use aides to relieve teachers of some of their routine duties — like monitoring lunchrooms and playgrounds. Special education and remedial programs may use aides to provide one-on-one drill and practice with students.

What You Might Be Doing

Since aides do not hold teaching licenses, they are not permitted by law to engage in teaching students, except under the direct supervision and in the presence of a teacher. Among the activities a classroom aide might be assigned are:

- Setting out class materials or helping to put them away;
- Working with one or more students on their assignments;
- Assisting students as they work with computers;
- Accompanying students as they move from place to place within the building;
- Carrying messages, paperwork, or lunch money to the school office;
- Monitoring student movement through the halls during class changes;

- Recording grades;
- Reading to students;
- Displaying student work on bulletin boards.

Probably the most common aide positions in elementary schools are those of lunchroom and playground aides. Their responsibilities revolve around keeping students safe and under control in school cafeterias and during lunch recess. A teacher or an administrator is assigned to be there as well, so the full responsibility for what can be a difficult job is not solely on the aide's shoulders.

Library aide is another common position in schools. As you might expect, the person holding this job may be assigned to putting books on shelves; cataloging books and materials; helping students find what they need; checking out materials; and reading to students. Since libraries have expanded to become media centers, these aides may also find themselves setting up and dismantling audio-visual equipment and working with computers.

Background and Skills Required

A college degree is not required for an aide position, although a high-school diploma may be. There are no universal requirements for these positions, so districts are free to establish their own. Some hire only district residents or give them first preference. In schools with large numbers of non-English speaking students, aides speaking the predominant language may be preferred. What is universal, however, is a requirement that aides be able to deal effectively with children.

Aide positions, because they are usually part-time and only for the school year, are often filled by mothers of young children who want to be home when their children are there. That's not to say others might not enjoy the work, however. As an aide, your pay will not be high. Your rewards will come more from the pleasure you draw from working with students.

Become a Teacher

One way to directly affect the public schools, albeit just one school at a time, is to become a teacher. If you are contemplating a career or a return to the workforce, teaching is a worthwhile avenue to explore. If you want to change career directions, you might seriously consider entering the teaching profession. Why? Because no other strategy described in this book will afford you the breadth of opportunities for making a difference in education. As a teacher, you will have immediate impact on the quality of education your students receive. As a faculty member, you will have a voice in determining what will be taught and how students will be treated. And as an educator, you can play a role in enhancing the entire profession. What's more, your career path can lead to school administration, which is where the power to affect widespread change lies.

How to Get There

You do not necessarily have to have a degree in education in order to teach in the public schools, but you do need a bachelor's degree of some kind (except for vocational teachers in some states). You will also have to be certified. In most states you will need:

A high-school diploma or GED certificate

A bachelor's degree

Courses on teaching methods, and other courses specific to individual states

Teaching experience, which may come through student teaching or an internship

Passage of one or more competency tests

A call to your state department of education's office of teacher certification will get you information on your state's requirements (see the Resources section for the phone number).

The types of teaching certificate awarded vary from state to state, but the trend is toward requiring higher standards for admittance to the profession. At the bottom of the certification ladder is the emergency certificate — granted to people who do not have the required coursework or experience, but who have essential skills in a subject for which there is a shortage of teachers. Math and science teachers sometimes are hired under this type of certificate. These teachers stand in danger of losing their jobs should the shortage ease before they acquire the prerequisites. The next level up is the provisional certificate, granted to beginning teachers. After these teachers have taught for a few years or have been granted tenure, they are usually given some sort of professional certificate. In some states, professional certificates have to be renewed periodically, perhaps after the acquisition of additional graduate school credits. The top-rung teaching certificate is the permanent license, which some states grant after a teacher has earned a certain number of graduate-level credits or a master's degree; others grant permanent licenses as soon as a probationary period has ended.

What if you already have a degree, but it's not in education? Can you still be certified? That depends on the individual state. Nearly thirty states now have "alternate routes," which allow college graduates to be hired as instructors as long as the hiring school district provides some kind of teacher mentoring program and the new teachers complete the missing course requirements within a specified period of time. Check with your state department of education's office of teacher certification to see if such a program is offered in your state.

If additional schooling is the only way you can get certified, you might want to consider programs, such as those at Harvard, George Washington University, and the University of California at Davis, that specialize in turning professionals from other fields into teachers. Or you could elect to get a traditional master's degree in education. Since many colleges and universities are moving toward requiring liberal arts degrees as part of five-year teacher-preparation programs, entry into an undergraduate teaching program may also be an option.

What You Can Expect to Be Doing

You have some idea of what it is like to be a teacher just from having observed them while you were in school. You know, for instance, that you will spend most of your time in a classroom, teaching and monitoring the work of students. But you will also have other roles to play. There are various "duties" — supervising on- and off-loading of buses; monitoring the playground, halls, and lunchroom; and creating bulletin board displays — which are often rotated among the teaching staff. Then there are such time-consuming but important activities as coaching and supervision of extracurricular activities (which you may volunteer for or be appointed to) and holding parent conferences. Finally, there are the activities you probably never saw because they frequently take place before and after school hours, out of the sight of students — attending faculty meetings and inservice training, grading papers, and preparing lesson plans. A teacher's day often lasts well beyond the hours the school is open.

Characteristics of a Good Teacher

Before you leap into the world of the classroom, you should be certain teaching is a field you will enjoy and be good at. You are likely to be a good teacher if you:

- Enjoy interacting with people;
- Feel comfortable in front of an audience;
- Find pleasure in helping people achieve their best;
- Know your field well;
- Have a good sense of humor;
- Understand yourself so you can understand others;
- Respect and trust others;
- Are willing to try new and various ways to convey information;
- Are adaptable to new situations and people;
- Are self-confident;
- Are able to handle being challenged by students;
- Are able to admit it when you're wrong;
- Are open to suggestions;
- Are unafraid of technology;
- Are enthusiastic;
- Are energetic;
- Are patient;
- Can manage time well;
- Can handle student discipline;
- Can keep your cool; and
- Can inspire others.

If this list frightens you, be assured that you needn't be a paragon of virtue to be a good teacher. You can have your "bad" days and be as subject to the frailties of the human condition as the next person. But these characteristics are those of the teachers students remember with fondness and respect.

What Kind of School Is for You?

When you look for a job as a teacher, you will learn that schools, even entire school districts, can be very different from one another. Some are more traditional in their approach to education than others. Some are formal; others are relaxed. You'll want to find those that support your educational philosophy, and provide the kind of atmosphere in which you feel most comfortable. Here are some questions you might want to ask yourself:

- Where do I want to teach? Am I tied to school districts near my home community or are there other places I would consider exploring? Do I prefer the comforts of a suburban district or the excitement and challenge of urban schools?

- What grade level do I want to teach? Do I love being around young children or am I more comfortable with older ones? Would I enjoy teaching a full range of subjects, as in primary classrooms, or would I prefer to teach only one or two?

- What kind of organizational structure would I be most comfortable in? Would I work best as part of a team? Would I find it stimulating to teach in an open classroom — one where a free flow of student activities is encouraged? Would I enjoy being part of a magnet school, where there is a specialized focus, such as science or the arts, and if so, what kind? Or would I prefer to start my teaching career in a traditional school?

- What kinds of students do I want to teach? Would a school that groups kids heterogeneously be preferable to one that divides them according to their abilities? Might I find working with special education students rewarding? Or the gifted and talented?

- Do I want to teach in a specialized school of some type, such as a school for the performing arts, a vocational-technical school, or an alternative school for students who haven't responded well to traditional schooling?

Your answers to these questions will help direct you toward colleges and courses to prepare you for teaching. If you decide you want to teach in city schools, for example, you might choose an urban college where your classmates are likely to be similarly inclined. If you want to teach special education classes, there are specialized courses you will need to take. Your answers will also point you toward the kinds of schools and school districts where you can best apply your skills.

When you're ready to start applying for jobs, ask for information about the district when you write or call for an application. If you are invited for an interview, ask to visit the schools where you might be assigned and talk with their teachers and administrators. Visit classrooms and observe how the staff members interact with students and with one another. You'll be able to pick up the tone and atmosphere in a school and use it to judge whether you want to work there. Also, use your interviews with prospective employers to find out as much about the schools and the school district as the interviewer learns about you. Even though positions may be hard to find, try to avoid taking a job that you know you will not enjoy or find fulfilling. You and your students deserve better.

Rewards

Most teachers will tell you they didn't go into teaching for the money. No one gets rich as a teacher. But salaries these days aren't that bad either. Since the 1970s, teacher salaries have been increasing at a rate well above that of inflation. While average starting salaries vary by state, most tend to be in mid-$20,000 range. With normal increments that come with each year of teaching and yearly increases in salary scales, teachers in a number of states with 20 years or more of service and a good number of credits under their belts can expect to earn $50-60,000 dollars for a ten-month year (the equivalent of $60-72,000 for twelve months). If you choose to coach or take on an extracurricular responsibility, you'll receive extra pay.

There are some nice fringe benefits, as well. Most school districts provide health insurance for their staffs, while some provide dental, life, and disability insurance and prescription drug plans as well.

Plus, you'll be part of a retirement system. And tenure, which is granted after working a certain number of years in a district (three is typical), offers teachers job security lacking in most other fields.

Vacation time is generous. In addition to all major holidays, most schools are closed for a week or so during the winter or spring and for two months in the summer. While there is some movement toward year-round schooling, old traditions are hard to break. Even if they no longer serve our non-agrarian society, today's vacation patterns are likely to remain in place in most districts.

Added to the extrinsic rewards of salary and benefits are the intrinsic rewards of personal satisfaction and pride. Teaching is an honored activity in this society. The profession's status can only increase as a result of such current trends as:

- reforms in teacher education to require more liberal arts courses, to raise admission criteria, or even to eliminate undergraduate programs;
- increased teacher competency and subject-matter testing;
- establishment of internship and induction programs; and
- requiring multiple evaluations of teaching performance.

Already, this increasing status is showing up in a commensurate increase in authority and responsibility. Efforts are underway throughout the country to involve teachers in making decisions that a few years ago would have been made for them by school boards and administrators.

The most valuable rewards, however, are those that come from interaction with students. Nothing can equal the sense of accomplishment that comes from having a successful former student tell you how much you influenced her. Or from watching a shy, hesitant kindergartener grow into a confident little boy. A paycheck is important, but no matter how big it is, it can't buy the joy found in the excited chatter and delighted smiles of a class of third graders watching a butterfly unfurl its wings for the first time. These are the moments that make teaching a truly worthwhile experience.

Section Three:
BACKGROUND
INFORMATION

How We Got to Where We Are Today:
A Brief History of Education

We accept free, public education as a given. It is our right as a citizen to receive it and our responsibility to fund it. But it wasn't always thus. Universal education wasn't achieved in the United States until this century and, even now, it isn't available in much of the third world.

We also tend to think that the enterprise we call public education has always been conducted as it is today, with schools organized into grades and divided into elementary, secondary, and college levels. A few senior citizens might remember the one-room schoolhouse with a teacher and no administrators, but most of us were educated in multi-room buildings by female teachers watched over by stern, male principals. Isn't that the way it always was?

No, it wasn't. The idea that all children should receive an education can be traced to the Protestant Reformation during the sixteenth century. Until that time, schooling was reserved for the sons of the aristocracy. But when the Reformation shifted the source of moral authority from the church to the Bible, being able to read became important. Entrance to heaven depended on knowing the truth, and to know the truth one had to be able to read the Bible. Martin Luther is said to have been the first advocate of compulsory education. He felt education was a matter for the state, and should not be left up to individual decision. Luther, however, never anticipated the divorce of schools — or the state — from church control, which is what eventually happened.

The Reformation, then, set into motion the forces that ultimately brought about the control of schools by civil authorities, and it was this system that was transplanted to Colonial America. But universal education took a long time to develop here and it didn't take root in all parts of the country at the same time.

American Education Before the 20th Century

New England was the birthplace of American public education. In 1635, Boston voted to establish a school supported by the income of a parcel of land set aside for that purpose and augmented by private subscriptions. By the end of the century, thirty other communities in New England had taken similar action. Thus originated the principle that towns should assume at least partial responsibility for financial support of schools.

The Puritans' emphasis on religion led to the first statutes requiring the establishment of schools. The "Old Deluder Satan" act passed by the Massachusetts colonial government in 1647 required all towns of 50 or more families to provide an elementary school-teacher, and towns of 100 or more families to establish a Latin grammar school for secondary education. Towns that refused to establish schools were assessed a fine. Along with these require-ments came the right to levy taxes in support of the schools. But since schools were expensive, many towns preferred to pay the fines. Even though the law was not widely obeyed, it did confirm the principle of education as a function of the state, and the town as the unit of administration.

Unlike New England, where education was acknowledged to be a civic responsibility, education in the Southern colonies was deemed a private affair. Reliance upon agriculture for a livelihood and, later, the plantation system, caused the population to be scattered over a wider area than was the case in New England. Also, there was more religious diversity among the colonists than existed in Puritan New England. Not only was it geographically difficult to create schools, there was no central force emphasizing the need to do so. A two-tier system developed in the South. Those who could afford to do so hired tutors and sent their children back to England for higher education. Orphans and children of the poor were required to take apprenticeships. Slave children, of course, were not educated at all.

The populations of the Middle Atlantic colonies were characterized by a wide diversity of religions and cultures. Since the density of those populations was much higher than in the South, schools sprang up. However, they were largely private schools, with each emphasizing its own ethnic, religious, and cultural values.

By the time of the American Revolution, all colonial legislatures had passed laws concerning education, but outside of New England they were not effective. Efforts to create public school systems were blocked in many places by various religious sects, each determined to operate its own denominational schools.

In 1785, under the Articles of Confederation, an ordinance providing for surveying public lands in the West directed that income from the sale of part of each section of land be used for common schools. A second ordinance, in 1787, carried this policy on to the land of the Northwest Territory. What could have been an enormous boon to education was often dissipated through corruption within state governments, but it did establish in each new state a tradition favoring public support for education.

During the westward advancement, the type of school system created depended on where the settlers were from. New England-style schools, supported by local taxes, appeared in Ohio, Michigan, and Indiana, while pauper schools developed in Mississippi and Alabama. Immigrants from Germany and other European countries brought with them their educational traditions as well. This diversity of traditions and the low population density led to a multiplicity of forms of schooling.

Beginning in the 1820s, there arose a reform movement which dramatically changed American education. Led mostly by citizens who were notables in their communities, the call was to create "common" schools: schools that were tuition free, universal, and nonsectarian. In New England, where schools had been "common" for generations, the emphasis was on upgrading the quality of education. In the Middle Atlantic region, the West, and the South (where the movement didn't catch on until after the Civil War), the focus was on establishing public schools. The reformers claimed that civic and moral values could be maintained only through a system of public education. By 1865, all states outside the South had achieved, or at least had begun to establish, universal, free, and tax-supported public schools.

American Education in the 20th Century

By 1900, the frontier had almost disappeared. More than two-fifths of the population was living in urban communities. Immigration was swelling the population. Child labor was common. Education was increasingly seen as a way to assimilate immigrants and to keep children out of factories. By 1918, all states had enacted compulsory school attendance laws.

In the years since, the number of students graduating from high school has been growing. In 1940, only about 38 percent of all 25 to 29 year olds had graduated from high school. In 1950, that number was almost 52 percent. Now that it is widely believed that everyone should have at least a high-school diploma, the number graduating has grown to almost 90 percent.

But the increased emphasis on a diploma is a two-edged sword. In the first half of this century and earlier, those who could not or would not meet academic standards still had job options available to them. Not as many, certainly, as those who completed their educations, but choices that would nevertheless allow them to support themselves and their families. That is not true today. Now a high-school diploma is the passport to getting all but the most menial of jobs.

How Schools Came to Be Managed As They Are

As the push for common schools and universal education took shape, a fundamental change occurred in the size of school districts and the way they were governed and managed. The responsibility for American education had gradually shifted from the family to society as a whole, acting through governmental agencies. Schools were organized into districts, each managed by local citizens. When the district consisted of one school, it was easy for the community to make decisions about the school collectively — to select the teacher, purchase books and supplies, and even build the school building. Later, as the population grew, these and many other decisions were delegated to committees that were an arm of the local government.

This system worked reasonably well in many places, especially in small towns and rural areas. But in some communities, primarily the cities, school boards became part of the political patronage system. As political scandals grew in frequency, a concerted effort was made to remove schools from the political process. In cities, this meant eliminating ward or community school boards and replacing them with one overall governing board — usually made up of citizens from the upper crust of society. In many areas, school boards were given the power to raise taxes independent of the local government, and laws were passed requiring that school boards be elected on a nonpartisan basis. One result of this reform effort, which took place over the early decades of this century, was to create larger school districts.

Around the same time as these changes in school governance, Frederick Taylor rose to prominence as a prophet of efficiency. His book, *The Principles of Scientific Management,* caught the interest of a generation of business and industry leaders and, since these people were the public-school decision-makers, it also had an influence on public education. The one-school district was "inefficient," so the move toward school consolidation, begun in an effort to depoliticize education, began to snowball. The advent of the school bus helped the process immeasurably. In 1900, when the national population stood at 72 million, there were approximately 110,000 school districts. By 1987, with a population of over 242 million, the number of districts had dropped to approximately 14,700.

As the size of school districts grew, school boards could no longer handle all the day-to-day administration of the schools. Originally hired as clerks and record keepers, a new breed of school manager began shaping the schools in the name of business efficiency. The influence of these managers grew beyond the bounds of local districts as they took on positions in fledgling state departments of education and started writing rules and regulations by which all schools in a state would have to operate.

The federal government played little role in education until after the Second World War. Then, faced with the facts that the draft had rejected five million potential inductees because of educational deficiencies and that the nation faced a critical shortage of teachers, Harry S. Truman became the first president to call for federal aid to education. In the late 1950s, Sputnik, the unmanned Soviet satellite, heightened the concern. Between 1958 and 1978, the percentage of federal support for education doubled in relation to the growth of state and local revenues. Federal and state courts also began to influence educational policy. In one landmark decision after another, they established rulings regarding school finance, desegregation, student rights of free speech, due process in suspensions, and elimination of institutional sexism.

Another, more recent, historical force has been the move from teacher professionalism to teacher unionization. By the mid-1960s, teachers had long been at the mercy of school boards and school administrators. The professionalization of school management had reduced the decision-making responsibility of teachers to that of making up lesson plans and dealing with day-to-day problems of educating a classroom of youngsters, often in far greater numbers than was considered educationally sound. Poor salaries were a widespread and chronic problem. Even though tenure had been instituted in most places to combat political machinations in school districts, unionization was an attractive option. So teachers began to turn their professional associations into labor organizations. The National Education Association and its state affiliates began to act more like a union, petitioning for bargaining rights and calling for strikes. The American Federation of Teachers took it a step further and became a member of the AFL-CIO. Both organizations successfully established bargaining units in many states and became strong lobbying forces at state and federal levels. Through labor negotiations and by weight of their influence on the political process, teachers now are a factor in educational decision-making at all levels.

Management philosophies have changed in the last two decades as well. With the United States' position as the world's industrial leader under threat, business and industry leaders are examining the way they organize and manage their workforces. Workers are being given greater latitude to make decisions about how the operation is run and how they carry out their jobs. At the same time, they are taking on greater responsibility for producing quality goods and services.

Just as schools adopted the business notion of efficiency in the early 1900s, they are now beginning to explore these new management theories and practices. Some districts, even some entire states, are experimenting with decentralized decision-making. School principals and their staffs, and sometimes parents as well, are being given greater authority to make decisions for their schools. Test results are being used — some say overused — as a measure of accountability.

Business is also the model for other ideas, principally the notion of free competition. If competing for customers works for business, competing for students will work for schools, say the proponents of this "voucher" system of education. Good schools will attract students, while poor schools will be forced to change or go out of business. Detractors point out that many parents lack the knowledge and the time to make wise choices among schools. Others charge that, if schools are allowed to select their students, those who are handicapped, disciplinary problems, or at the bottom of the academic heap may wind up in some "dumping ground" for unwanted students. The argument is far from over.

How Curriculum and Instruction Evolved

Just as school governance has changed over the years, so have ideas and convictions about the purpose of schools. The "Old Deluder Satan" act explicitly stated that the purpose of education in colonial New England was to teach children to read and understand religious principles and capital laws. The common-school proponents saw schools as a mechanism for conveying the civic and moral values of society. But as the population grew and became more diverse, clarity of purpose became blurred. There was, and still is, great faith in the power of public schooling to correct society's ills by improving individuals, to reform society not by direct means but by changing the next generation. If drug usage is a problem, drug and alcohol programs are introduced into the schools; if the carnage on our highways is too great, driver education programs are started; if the rate of illegitimate births is high, family life education is added to the curriculum. Schools have become conglomerates, much like businesses. From time to time, people decry this piling on of responsibilities and demand a "back to basics" approach. But no one seems to know how to address the ills of society without some involvement of the schools.

As the purpose of schooling has changed, so has its content. High schools, for instance, have changed dramatically. At the turn of this century, as great waves of immigration swept over the United States, public high schools faced an influx of new students. Up until then, high schools were attended almost exclusively by young men intent upon attending a college or university. The response of some educators to the new students, most of whom had no plans to continue their formal education beyond high school, was to cling firmly to the precepts of a classical education for all. These educators believed that Latin, Greek, mathematics, English, German, French, history, and the sciences were just as appropriate for their new students as they had been for their predecessors. In 1893, Nicholas Murray Butler, then president of Columbia University, and Charles W. Eliot, who was president of Harvard University, expressed the view that "Every subject which is taught at all in a secondary school should be taught in the same way and to the same extent to every pupil so long as he pursues it, no matter what the probable destination of the pupil may be, or at what point his education is to cease."[23]

By World War II, that view had been suppressed in favor of an increased emphasis on preparing students for the world of work. Vocational education programs were instituted. Courses considered more relevant to student life outside the classroom replaced traditional subjects for students not preparing for higher education. Schools developed three levels of study — college-bound, vocational, and general studies. Most of today's adults are familiar with this system, but it is not without critics. Today's call for higher standards is sometimes accompanied by demands for return to a "common" curriculum — one grounded in or limited to language, literature, fine arts, mathematics, natural sciences, history, geography, and social studies. We seem to be coming full circle.

Teaching techniques have changed also. Rote memorization was the favored learning technique of many earlier cultures, and that approach was carried over to colonial America. Discipline was rigid: "Spare the rod and spoil the child" was the central axiom of schooling. But both ideas were turned on their ears in the late 1800s by John Dewey, who advocated schools based on such progressive education precepts as:

- Children are different from one another, and their individual differences must be recognized;

- Children learn what they are interested in learning and they do it best by being actively engaged in their own learning;
- Education does not occur only within the walls of a classroom — schools must incorporate the larger world;
- Classrooms should be laboratories for democracy;
- Social goals, as well as intellectual goals, are important;
- A child must be taught to think critically rather than to accept blindly.

When Dewey, his wife, and several neighbors created their school in 1896, it shocked most educators of the day. But within 25 years, at least 50 new schools based on the same principles had been formed. Not everyone accepted Dewey's notions, however. Bitter controversies developed between his progressive followers and their critics. Conservatives accused progressive schools of coddling pupils and catering to their transient interests. They decried the lack of discipline and claimed that students failed to grasp fundamentals.

But Dewey's ideas eventually became part of the mainstream. Students were encouraged to experiment with ideas and relate them to their lives. Class discussion became common. Team teaching, where three or four teachers have joint responsibility for groups of eighty to a hundred students, was instituted in many schools, and some schools literally tore down walls separating classrooms to create more flexible learning spaces. Grading, especially at the elementary-school level, came to be based on individual achievement rather than comparison with other students. Innovative teachers developed programs that integrated several parts of the curriculum. A multi-disciplinary project, for instance, might have a group of seventh or eighth graders study a particular culture, create and bury artifacts that represent that culture, and then unearth and analyze another group's work. A far cry from the reading, writing, and recitation regimen of more traditional schooling.

Dewey's ideas — although few still recognize them as his — have had tremendous influence on the educational practices of today. Education conservatives, however, are still blaming his ideas for the academic failures of students. Their cry for a return to more formal approaches is still being heard and acted upon. Things change, yet remain the same.

Efforts to Improve Today's Schools

Today's schools hardly resemble the schools of fifty years ago, even though, in many places, the buildings housing them are the same. If you haven't been in a classroom for some time, you might be surprised at some of the things going on there. Technology has moved in. With information growing exponentially, there is no way to keep up without the use of computers. Schools that can afford them — there's the hitch — are providing them to students to track down information in computer-stored encyclopedias, brush up on skills and knowledge (computers are very patient tutors), and produce reports that can include color graphics and charts. Teachers use computers to monitor student progress and keep records.

Some elementary schools are no longer divided into grades. The state of Kentucky, for instance, has called for the institution of non-graded classes as part of its effort to improve schools. The new mixed-age classes group students according to how skilled they are in particular subjects, such as reading and math. A seven-year-old having difficulty grasping math concepts but doing better than average in reading, may be grouped with six-year-olds for math instruction and eight-year-olds for reading. Since children learn at different rates, the advantage in this system is that students are always receiving instruction appropriate for them and are working with other children of similar ability.

Having students learn with and from each other is gaining favor in many classrooms — high school as well as elementary. Known as cooperative learning, the idea is for groups of students to work together to make sure everyone understands the information. Researchers have demonstrated that kids who work in groups learn better than those who struggle on their own. What's more, slower-learning students make big gains in achievement without holding back their brighter, more knowledgeable peers.

Elementary math instruction has also changed. Memorization of formulas has been replaced by hands-on experience. Students are given everyday objects to count, combine, subtract, and divide. Then they are given real-life problems to solve and encouraged to use whatever they need to arrive at solutions. The emphasis is on understanding math concepts, not just following procedures.

But while today's schools are different and, in many ways, better than earlier versions, they don't always reach the goal of educating all children to the highest level of their abilities. So there are continuing efforts to improve them. The 1983 publication of the report of the National Commission on Excellence in Education, *A Nation at Risk,* sparked states to increase aid to education, set higher high-school graduation standards, institute state-wide testing, require changes in teacher training and licensing, establish career ladders for teachers, and raise teacher salaries. Some states have imposed "no pass, no play" rules for high-school athletes, while others have taken away the driving privileges of dropouts. Failing school districts have sometimes been taken over and run by state agencies or, in at least one case (in Chelsea, Massachusetts), by a university.

Improving the public schools is also on the national agenda. In 1990, President Bush and the nation's governors established six national goals for education. By the year 2000, they said,

- all children in America will start school ready to learn;
- the high-school graduation rate will increase to at least 90 percent;
- American students will leave grades 4, 8, and 12 having demonstrated competency in challenging subject matter, including English, mathematics, science, history, and geography;
- American students will be first in the world in mathematics and science achievement;
- every adult American will be literate and will possess the skills necessary to compete in a global economy and to exercise the rights and responsibilities of citizenship;
- every school in America will be free of drugs and violence and will offer a disciplined environment conducive to learning.

To meet these goals, the U. S. Department of Education established the America 2000 program (recently renamed "Goals 2000: Educate America" by Clinton administration appointees). It challenges communities to:

- adopt the six national goals;
- develop community-wide strategies to meet them;

- design a report card to measure progress; and
- plan for and support what the Department is calling New American Schools.

The U.S. Department of Education also created a non-profit, privately funded New American Schools Development Corporation (NASDC) and recruited business leaders from some of the country's largest corporations to serve on its board of directors. The purpose of the corporation is to rethink the way American children are educated. To do so, in the summer of 1991, NASDC issued a call for proposals from those interested in meeting three challenges: to seek funda-mental institutional change in American schooling; to do so while operating on a budget comparable to that of conventional schools; and to have students meet new national standards in mathematics, science, English, history, and geography, while preparing them for responsible citizenship, further learning, and productive employment.[24] Nearly 700 proposals were received, of which eleven were selected to share in the $200 million NASDC is planning to award over a five-year period. While NASDC's failure to meet some of its fundraising targets in 1992 led some observers to doubt whether its New American Schools would ever see the light of day,[25] the eleven winning proposals still may point to future directions in education:[26]

> **ATLAS Communities.** This program is a collaborative effort among Apple Computer, IBM, AT&T, the National Alliance of Business, and three well-known educational reformers: James Comer of Yale, Howard Gardner of Harvard, and Theodore Sizer of Brown. It will serve grades pre-kindergarten through 12 in urban, suburban, and rural communities in Lancaster, Pennsylvania; Norfolk, Virginia; Prince Georges County, Maryland; and Gorham, Maine. The emphasis will be on active learning within a clearly focused curriculum. Adults will work with students over periods longer than a year. The project will be managed by teams that include teachers, parents, students, administrators, and other community and school professionals.

> **Bensenville Community.** This community of 17,000 outside of Chicago plans to turn its entire town into a campus, and its schools into life-long learning centers. A team of 23 local people — the village manager, a day-care director, a pastor, a

pharmacist, local business owners, parents, students, teachers, and administrators designed a program where schooling will become year-round, with flexible scheduling. Courses will be multi-disciplinary, and work will be evaluated through performance portfolios instead of traditional tests and grades. Student progress will be based on three achievement levels — whether the student exceeds, meets, or does not meet world-class standards. Community meetings will be used as one technique for reporting school progress. Technology will be used extensively. A governing body, consisting of parents, business leaders, government officials, educators, and other citizens, will be required to participate in ongoing training.

Community Learning Centers of Minnesota. This project takes advantage of a Minnesota law allowing teachers to contract with school boards to start their own schools, with the understanding that their "charter" will be revoked if students do not meet agreed-upon standards. Teachers will hold full responsibility for designing curricula, arranging staff training, supervising para-professional personnel, and reviewing each other's performance. Councils made up of teachers, students, parents, and community members will manage each of the three initial sites. The intent is for the program to spread throughout the state.

Modern Red Schoolhouse. School districts in Indiana, Charlotte-Mecklenburg, North Carolina, and Kayenta, Arizona, are part of this program headed by William Bennett, former U.S. secretary of education. The emphasis will be on a classical education curriculum bolstered by technology. Individual education contracts will be developed with and by students, who will advance through their studies at their own pace.

Audrey Cohen College. From seven to thirty schools in Arizona, California, Illinois, Mississippi, New York City, and Washington, DC, will participate in this program. Each semester, students will focus on "a major purpose," which combines "a substantive body of knowledge and a socially important thrust," and then apply what they learn. Core subjects will relate to each semester's purpose, and technology will be used by students to gather and analyze information. The project was designed by individuals associated with museums, foundations, and national organizations, as well as educators and business people.

Los Angeles Learning Centers. Two inner-city sites — one built "from scratch" and one encompassing an existing high school and its feeder schools — will participate in the pilot phase of this project. Interdisciplinary teams, including community members, will be responsible for teaching in these nongraded schools. Each student will be linked with an older student, a teacher, and the student's parents or a community volunteer in a partnership that will last several years. Schools will be open from dawn until late evening, fifty weeks a year. Decisions about budgets, personnel, curriculum, and other aspects of school life will be made by a council of teachers, parents, students, and the principal. Outcomes will be assessed through standard tests, student portfolios, and international comparisons. Five corporations — ARCO, Bank of America, GTE California, Rockwell International, and the Times-Mirror Company — joined the United Teachers of Los Angeles, the Los Angeles Educational Partnership (a business-led organization), and the Los Angeles Unified School District in sponsoring the program.

Roots and Wings. An emphasis on prevention and early-intervention strategies to keep students from ever needing special education or long-term remediation is the hallmark of this program, which will serve children from birth to age eleven, many of them from low-income families, in four communities in St. Mary's County, Maryland. "Roots" refers to the program's goal of building a strong foundation in basic skills; "wings" are the expectation that every child will meet world-class standards in English, mathematics, science, history, and geography. Cooperative learning and group investigation are strong components of the program, which is based, in part, on more than two decades of research conducted by Robert Slavin and his colleagues at Johns Hopkins University's Center for Research on Effective Schooling for Disadvantaged Students. Schools will serve as family support centers where services such as health, mental health, day-care, adult education, and food- and rent-assistance will be available.

Expeditionary Learning. Outward Bound, USA, along with six partners, is sponsoring this program, which will operate in schools in Portland, Maine; Boston; New York City; Decatur, Georgia; and Douglas County, Colorado; plus in a new "charter" school set up for this purpose. Students will engage in various experiential, intellectual, or service "expeditions." To attain a diploma, they will have to complete a rigorous "world-class curriculum," pass the International Baccalaureate examination, and carry out an approved senior service expedition. Service projects, such as recycling centers and day-care facilities, will be offered on site. Professional staff will be augmented by residencies offered to artists, professionals, and scholars.

National Alliance for Restructuring Education. A long list of organizations, including Apple Computer, Xerox Corporation, the National Alliance of Business, the National Center on Education and the Economy, and the Center for the Study of Social Policy are behind this project. It seeks to define school outcomes and measures of progress toward them, and to identify strategies that will foster public support for higher standards and the changes in policy and practice that will be required to achieve them. It will provide technical assistance in the states of Arkansas, Kentucky, New York, Vermont, and Washington and in the cities of Pittsburgh, San Diego, Rochester, and White Plains, New York.

The Co-NECT School. Technology is the emphasis of this project, lead by a Boston-based consulting organization and its six partners (Apple Computer, NYNEX, Lotus Development Corporation, the Massachusetts Corporation for Education Telecommunications, Earthwatch, Inc., and the Boston College Center for the Study of Testing, Evaluation, and Educational Policy). It is targeted at inner-city, at-risk students, and the initial sites are elementary schools in Boston and Worcester, Massachusetts. Clusters of six teachers and one hundred students will stay together for several years, supported by a computer-based communications network connecting them to each other and to learning resources. The curriculum will focus heavily on science and math learned through projects and seminars and with the aid of computers, multimedia, and interactive video.

Odyssey Project. This project plans to operate year-round, dawn-to-dusk learning centers in the fifty-four schools of Gaston County, North Carolina. Students will move through the centers based on their completion of defined outcomes, measured quantitatively and qualitatively. Students will be required to perform community service. Parent participation will be encouraged, and health and social services will be available.

Parent and Community Involvement

The involvement of parents and other community members in several of these programs will take the form of school-site councils, the decision-making forum of an increasingly popular method of governing schools, variously called school-based management, site-based management, or decentralized decision-making. A few states — Florida, Kentucky, and South Carolina, for instance — have mandated school-site councils as part of their reform efforts, although the authority granted them varies from state to state. Illinois has taken the notion a step further by vesting the majority of decision-making power, including budget control, in Chicago's school-site councils. In other places, school-based management is being implemented at the discretion of the local district — Santa Fe, New Mexico; Hoboken, New Jersey; New York City; Allentown, Pennsylvania; and Prince Georges County, Virginia, to name a few. Here, too, the range of decisions being made by councils varies. Some school boards have granted broad discretionary power to their schools, while others allow councils only a restricted range of decisions. The most effective school-based management occurs where there are mechanisms, such as waivers from district policies and union contracts, that permit implementation of innovative faculty- and community-supported initiatives.

The philosophy behind school-based management is that the people closest to where teaching and learning are taking place, are the ones best equipped to make operational decisions. These decisions can include curriculum, staffing, building maintenance, and the purchase of textbooks and other materials. Schools operating under the direction of school councils are held accountable for meeting district goals and standards by their school boards and central office administrations.

While districts and schools vary in how they implement this process, those that work the best share some common features. They all have school-site councils where decision-making is shared among the principal, teachers, parents, community members, and sometimes students; they have clear agreements with their boards of education about which decisions the councils are authorized to make; they all operate within the dictates of law, regulations, and local board policy (although special exceptions can be granted); and they have some autonomy in budgeting and spending funds.

Boards of education and central office administrators continue to control such things as the establishment of attendance zones, promotion standards, attendance requirements, and local graduation requirements. They also set the tone for the district and shape the expectations and work norms of the staff, negotiate collective bargaining agreements and enforce contracts, and raise and allocate revenue.

Since school-based management is a recent practice, little is known about its impact on student outcomes. Its success or failure will depend on how willing state departments of education, local boards of education, and school administrators are to share their considerable power, and how forcefully school-site councils take hold of their opportunities and build community support for their efforts. It is an important development in our system of education, however, because it allows all those interested in their schools to have a greater voice in how they are run. For more on councils, see pages 70-73.

Effective Schools

You probably have a picture in your mind of what a "good" school looks like. More than likely, that picture is based on the schools you attended and how you felt about them. If stern discipline, for instance, was the norm in the elementary school you attended and you felt confined by it, you may think good schools are those that are more child-centered. If, however, you are grateful for the limits discipline put on you and your peers, you may define good schools as those that impose similar controls on today's students. It's only human nature to define "good" and "bad" according to our own experiences and beliefs.

But there is also a body of information gleaned from research on what constitutes an "effective" school, i.e., one where all students — regardless of who their parents are or where they live — are performing at their grade level or above. Most of these findings have been accepted by educators all across the country, so it is likely the schools in your community are attempting to model themselves after them. You may want to use these characteristics as well in judging and becoming involved with schools in your community.

Good schools are those where *all* students learn. While this may appear to be self-evident, you'd be surprised at the number of teachers and administrators who make excuses about why some of their students are achieving and others not. "Some of them just aren't as bright as others," is one explanation. True, but all children of normal intelligence can learn, provided they are motivated and given the right opportunities. It may take longer for some, but good teachers compensate for diverse learning styles by using multiple techniques to present information. They also actively engage their students in a collaborative learning process, unlike some schooling that makes learning a passive, isolated experience.

"Some kids come from homes that keep them from learning," is another frequently heard excuse. In a 1992 Metropolitan Life Insurance Company survey, teachers ranked disinterested parents as the number one reason their students were unprepared to learn.[27] There is a kernel of truth to this. Children from families where education is not particularly valued are harder for teachers to reach.

But that's not a sufficient reason to give up on children. There are ways that schools can reach out to them and their families. There might be adults in those children's lives who want the children to do well in school, but just don't know how to help them. With the right message, these adults can be brought into the equation.

You can tell whether your schools have high expectations for all their students by looking for such practices as:

- Teachers expressing the belief that all students can master the curriculum and speaking well of each other and their students;

- Instructional groups being formed and re-formed frequently, so that children are not rigidly grouped by ability levels;

- Teachers using a variety of approaches, including ones where children of different abilities work together, and trying new ones if skills are not being mastered;

- Students being given recognition for their efforts as well as their achievements, and provided with opportunities to accept responsibility and be leaders.

Good schools focus on student achievement. Time is a valuable commodity in effective schools. "Fooling around" by students is kept to a minimum so teachers can use every minute possible for instruction. Fun activities, such as field trips, are an extension of the curriculum, not time away from learning. Administrators also make a concerted effort to protect instructional time. For instance, school-wide assemblies are held only on very special occasions, and announcements over the school's loudspeaker are restricted to the very beginning and end of the school day.

Testing is a regular part of the school program. School staff monitor student performance closely, not so much to judge students as to determine program weaknesses and to identify ineffective teaching practices. They believe that student failure is their problem as much as it is the students'. Staff development activities are held regularly to help teachers improve their skills.

If your school has a proper emphasis on instruction and learning, you should be able to see such signs as:

- Homework that is regularly assigned and promptly checked;

- Teachers spending substantial class time in active and direct instruction;

- Teachers using a variety of techniques to measure student progress (such as homework, tests, question-and-answer sessions, and class discussions), and then giving students prompt feedback on classwork and test results;

- Consistent standards for promotion that are well understood by teachers, students, and parents;

- A requirement that students master the skills of one level before they are allowed to move on to the next;

- Test results fully reported to the entire community in ways that allow comparison with other schools.

Good schools have good principals. These principals are strong leaders: when they see a need, they assume responsibility for meeting it, then take action by organizing what needs to be done and inspiring others to help. They make themselves visible and accessible, take an active role in supervising teachers, and articulate a clear and positive philosophy of education. They are strong, but not domineering leaders. They respect their staffs, but they also monitor them, hold them accountable, and give them frequent feedback on how well they and the school are doing. Effective principals can be recognized through their:

- Ambitious goals;

- Frequent discussions with staff about student achievement and instructional strategies, and reviews of lesson plans;

- Insistence that tests and instructional materials match the school's curriculum;

- Involvement of everyone who will be affected, before making a decision;

- Emphasis on parent and community involvement;

- Provision of staff development opportunities, keyed to meet instructional needs;

- Ability to focus limited resources — human and monetary — to the best advantage of students.

Good schools involve school staff, parents, and other community members in school improvement. Schools that are part of the community are stronger than those isolated from it; they enjoy better reputations and stronger financial support. And research shows that students whose parents are involved in their education do better in school, and that schools where parents and community are involved are more effective. School personnel foster involvement by making visitors feel welcome. School policies about such things as discipline, homework, promotion, testing, and ability grouping are discussed openly and jointly modified. Parents and the community participate in structured ways, such as committees or school councils, in developing goals and making decisions about the school.

Good home-school-community relations are evident when:

- There is an organized parent group that the school fully supports by providing it with meeting space, information about the instructional program, and access to school equipment, such as copiers;
- The school regularly communicates with parents and the community through newsletters, home visits, phone calls, notes, and parent-teacher conferences;
- The school and classrooms are open to parents and other responsible community members.

Good schools are pleasant, safe, and orderly places. There is a school-wide approach to discipline where rules are clear. The emphasis is on self-discipline. Students are held responsible for orderly behavior in halls and classrooms; teachers for staying on schedule and for using effective instructional techniques; custodians for keeping the building clean and in good repair; and administrators for monitoring all school activities. When students fail to keep up their end of the bargain, they are called to task. So are teachers and other school staff, albeit in a different way. There are no slackers in good schools.

The noise in a good school is the noise of active learning. Teachers and students are not worried about their personal safety. The physical facilities may not be new, but there is sufficient workspace, and it is clean and attractive. There are sufficient supplies and equipment to carry out the learning program.

Other indications of a positive environment are:

- Students and teachers treating each other with respect;
- Students being given regular and frequent recognition for positive behavior;

- Teachers who are good models of behavior and academic commitment;

- Parents being quickly notified if their children develop problems;

- No evidence of drug use among students or faculty;

- Effective monitoring of entrances and hallways to prevent disruption by outsiders;

- Community support for school budgets and other referenda.

Good schools make effective use of constructive educational influences in the community. Educational influences are everywhere, not just in schools. Families, churches, television, street gangs, youth agencies, the business community, libraries — all influence youngsters, for good or ill. Effective schools reach out into their communities and work with constructive elements to influence students to learn in positive ways.

Some schools have become centers of their communities. Adult education classes are held there, both during the day and in the evening. Before- and after-school recreational programs are provided; day-care may be available as well. Health and social welfare services can be obtained in the building. There may even be a "parents room," where people can gather for meetings or just to chat. The feeling that this is "my school" is not confined to just teachers and students.

Other indications of effective use of community resources include:

- Churches and other religious institutions emphasizing the importance of education, and religious leaders using their influence to get their congregations involved in the schools;

- Businesses providing work-study programs for students;

- Local police conducting drug-awareness programs;

- School/business partnerships and school volunteer programs bringing business people and others from the community into the school to share their expertise and knowledge;

- Collaborative programs with health and social service providers for students and their families.

Every community wants good schools for its children, but it takes community support to achieve them. It is hard, however, to develop community support when there are conflicting ideas about what constitutes good schooling. Educators and the general public alike often disagree on particulars and priorities. The research on effective schools can serve as a starting point for reaching consensus because it is so well known and well accepted among teachers and administrators and because, in many ways, it confirms the public's beliefs about the characteristics of good schools.

What Americans Think About Their Schools

Do your ideas about public schools match those of your fellow Americans? Here are some results from the 23rd (1991) and 24th (1992) annual Gallup/Phi Delta Kappa polls of the public's attitudes toward public schools.[28]

Curriculum and Testing

Substantial majorities of Americans believe schools (and students) should be held to a set of standards that have been accepted nationwide. Sixty-eight percent say the public schools in their communities should be required to use a standardized national curriculum and 81 percent would require their schools to conform to national achievement standards and goals. Seventy-one percent favor requiring their schools to use standardized, national tests. The tests would measure academic achievement, but should also be used to:

- rank local public schools in terms of student achievement (65 percent);

- identify areas where teachers need to improve their teaching skills (79 percent);

- identify areas where students need extra help (85 percent); and

- determine whether students advance to the next grade (60 percent).

The movement toward national standards has been building momentum for the last several years. The National Council of Teachers of Mathematics has already prepared standards for that discipline, and efforts are underway to develop national standards in science, history, arts, civics, geography, and English. See the Resources section for names and addresses of the organizations developing them.

The educational community has offered more than a little resistance to adopting national standards. Opponents fear that the flexibility needed to meet local community expectations and needs of individual children will be lost if there is a single set of standards. Do all high-school graduates need to know calculus, for instance?

Will learning-disabled children be denied diplomas? These are the kinds of questions they ask. Proponents, however, argue that national standards and curricula are necessary in order to determine whether all children are getting an adequate education.

The research on effective schools, discussed in the previous section, does not speak to the issue of national standards; it only points to the need for high standards and a belief that all students can acquire the basic skills, given enough time and effective teaching. This research recognizes standardized tests as a valuable assessment tool, so long as they measure what is being taught.

School Governance and Operation

Substantial majorities of Americans question fundamental features of the way today's school systems are run. Sixty-two percent think districts should allow students to attend any public school in the community, regardless of where they live. They believe the most important criteria in choosing a school are the quality of teaching staff (85 percent), maintenance of student discipline (76 percent), the courses offered (74 percent), and the size of classes (57 percent).

Improvement would also come about, seventy-six percent of Americans say, if teachers and principals were given greater say in how their schools are run. Seventy-nine percent would rather have school district policy decisions made by councils of teachers, principals, and parents than by school boards and administrators.

The traditional school year, and even the traditional uses of school buildings, need rethinking, Americans believe. Fifty-five percent favor extending the school year by 30 days, with three-week vacation breaks evenly distributed throughout the year. Seventy-seven percent think school buildings should become community centers, offering health and social welfare services, as well as educational services, for children and their families.

Some of these opinions are supported by research. Class size, for instance, does make a difference. A recent Tennessee study demonstrated that students in small classes (13 to 17 students per teacher) did better on standardized tests, no matter where they lived — inner-city, suburban, urban, or rural areas.[29] However, in order to make the best use of reduced class-sizes, teachers had to be trained in how to work with small groups. Small class-sizes may be important, but achieving them in all schools would require a large infusion of money.

The importance of school discipline is also supported by the research on effective schools. Clearly, students cannot learn where there is continual disruption and where staff and students are fearful for their safety. The problem is how to achieve good discipline and protect students and teachers in neighborhoods plagued by drugs and criminal behavior. The solution to these societal problems, of course, goes far beyond the individual school. They have to be addressed on many levels — local, state, and national — and through many sources — legislatures, police, courts, schools, social services — but that is not an excuse for throwing in the towel. Individuals can make a difference; schools in high-crime areas have become refuges from the world outside. It takes determination by school personnel, of course. It also takes the help of concerned citizens who are willing to take such actions as pressuring city government for greater police protection, setting up neighborhood watches to discourage drug dealing and robbery, and providing "safe houses" for children who feel in danger on the street.

School choice is another one of the "hot" issues in education, although not nearly as incendiary when it is applied to public schools only. There have been a number of attempts to create programs where parents and students can choose a public school other than the one in their neighborhood; some have failed and some have succeeded. Tough questions, such as how schools will be financed and how transportation will be arranged, have to be answered before inter-district choice (which some people are suggesting) can become a reality.

Extending the school year is an educationally sound idea. Other countries — notably Japan — keep students in school longer than we do. The more instruction a student experiences, the more he or she is likely to learn. American teachers have long complained that their students lose ground over the summer and have to be drilled in previously taught concepts every fall. But parents have consistently resisted having their children in school year-round. The tradition of long summer vacations is hard to break, even though its genesis was in an agrarian society's need to have family help with crops. Change comes hard.

School Finance

Americans believe in equity — 80 percent say that the amount of money allocated to public education in their states should be the same for all students, whether they live in wealthy or poor school districts; 62 percent favor court action to equalize spending per pupil where it is found to be unequal. By a margin of 55 percent to 40 percent, they are even willing to have a one-percent increase in the state sales tax to raise money for education.

Fifty-four percent of Americans think teachers are underpaid and favor raising their salaries, while 32 percent oppose such a move. If it were necessary to cut school costs, only 15 percent of Americans would want to reduce the number of teachers, while 47 percent would freeze all salaries, and 73 percent would reduce the number of administrators.

Fifty-five percent of Americans say public schools should make preschool programs available to 3- and 4-year-olds and, by a narrow 49 percent to 42 percent margin, say they are willing to pay more taxes to fund free preschool programs for children from low-income families.

These opinions are somewhat startling, given most Americans' strong resistance to increasing taxes, especially when the revenues are to be used in communities other than their own. In fact, fiscal equity may be more of an ideal than something people are willing to support with their taxes, if the experiences of states that have had to rework their educational finance systems are any example. Typically, any lawsuit aimed at forcing equity has been bitterly fought by state governments, and court orders to set up more equitable funding methods have created consternation among legislators unwilling to take unpopular actions. You may be aware of some of the arguments if you live in one of the states that have had their school funding systems challenged:

Finance systems ruled unconstitutional

California
New Jersey
Connecticut
Washington
Wyoming
West Virginia
Arkansas
Kentucky
Montana
Texas
Missouri

Finance systems under challenge

Idaho
Michigan
Oklahoma
Oregon
Alabama
Illinois
Indiana
Kansas
Massachusetts
Minnesota
North Dakota
Rhode Island
Tennessee

Source: Phi Delta Kappan, *September 1991, p. 52 (updated).*

Perhaps you don't agree with all of the opinions expressed in the Gallup Poll. After all, just because a majority of Americans believe something, it isn't necessarily true or right. But polling data does show you which of your favorite issues you are likely to find community support for and which ones you are not.

Information to Make Your Efforts More Effective

The more you know about the way schools are organized and how they function, the more effective you will be in your efforts to assist or reform them. Here's some basic information you need to know.

How Public Education Is Organized

"We can't do anything about that." "That's a decision I'm not authorized to make." Those are two of the most frustrating responses anyone seeking action can hear. If you are looking to make some sort of change in your district's policies or practices and you run into that kind of roadblock, to counter it you'll need to know where different kinds of educational decisions are made.

Let's assume your district is concerned about the high cost of remedial and special education programs (even a few special education students can be very expensive for a small district) and wants to know how costs can be controlled without causing educational damage to the children involved. Let's also assume you have been appointed to serve on a board of education advisory committee to investigate the issue and that you are a neophyte when it comes to public education.

One of the first things you and the committee will want to determine is where the various laws and regulations governing remedial and special education originated — at the federal, state, or local levels. Since there are numerous state and federal mandates covering these areas, you might also want to know which agency formulated them, so you'll know where to go for information. If certain policies were the result of local decisions, it will also be helpful to know who has the authority to change them. Would any alterations have to be approved by the board of education or could they be accomplished by administrative decree? To help you find your way through this thicket, you should know how public schools are organized.

The U.S. Constitution says nothing about schools; therefore, the responsibility for education is left to the states. The federal government does provide some money, however, and even though the amount is small in comparison to education's other funding sources, where there is money there is also control. In addition, the federal government does have jurisdiction over civil rights, which has led to laws and regulations about discrimination and the provision of special education. And the President and the Secretary of Education can wield enormous influence over the direction of public education through the use of their positions as bully pulpits — speaking out about issues of concern to the administration in power.

But the primary responsibility for educating America's children lies with the states. Each handles the function differently, but all delegate it to subunits of government called school districts. In some states, these districts correspond to county lines, in others they are coterminous with municipal boundaries, in still others they may be regional in nature, taking in several municipalities. Hawaii is unusual in that the state has only one school district.

All states have delegated at least some authority to local districts and what are called boards of education, boards of school trustees, or school committees. These boards evolved out of the time in our country's history when parents would band together to build a school, hire a teacher, and buy books and supplies in order to provide education for their children. The principle of lay control of education continued even after education became the responsibility of state government (for more on the history of education in the United States, see pages 134-150). The decisions boards are authorized to make vary from state to state. All are charged with selecting textbooks, for instance, but in states such as Texas and California, local boards can choose only those that have been first approved by state authorities (which, incidentally, gives those states enormous influence over textbook content.)

In most cases, boards of education are elected; only three percent, typically urban boards, are appointed by other elected officials. Both methods have their advantages and drawbacks. Elected boards are directly responsible to their constituents, for instance, but appointed boards are less likely to get into battles with municipal officials or whoever appointed them. Appointed boards also offer an opportunity — but by no means a guarantee — of greater representation by minority groups. Similarly, there are arguments for and against paying board members for attending meetings. Thirty-two states allow some form of compensation, but in most of them only a few districts — generally those serving urban areas — actually provide payment. Virtually all board members receive reimbursement for expenses incurred in carrying out their duties.

The sources of funding for education also vary from state to state. State coffers provide nearly the entire school budget in some states, leaving little, if any, to come from local sources. Most, however, rely heavily on local property taxes, which has led to inequalities in educational opportunity. Localities with businesses that provide most of the property tax revenue can allot more for their schools with less cost to individual taxpayers than can districts that depend on homeowners for the majority of their revenue. These inequalities have led to court decisions overturning education funding systems in 11 states, with 13 others currently under challenge (see table on page 161).

For information about how education is organized in your state, consult your public library or call your state department of education (see Resources section for phone numbers). Your library will also have reference books and data about the state's schools. Your local newspaper covers stories about your community's schools and board of education. It's a good source for gathering information about how your district works.

State Statutes and Regulations

If you set off to find out about a particular aspect of your schools, whether it is on your own or as a member of a committee, you are likely to run into someone who will tell you that "the state requires we do it this way." If you do, it might help to know the key laws, court decisions, and education department regulations in your state. For instance, depending on what your interest is, you might want to ask:

- Does your state require special certification for various types of teaching positions? Do all teachers in those specialties hold certificates? (There is often a loophole allowing "temporary" certificates for hard-to-fill positions.)

- Does your state require negotiated teacher contracts? May teachers go on strike if negotiations bog down? If collective bargaining isn't allowed, how are salaries determined?

- Is tenure granted? Who gets it? Just teachers? Teachers and administrators? After how many years?

- Are textbooks chosen at the state level? What is the process for selecting them?

- What courses does your state mandate? Are there exemptions for certain students?

- Are state tests administered? In what grades? To all students? Does failure trigger required remediation? Is passage of a particular test required for graduation?

- Does your state issue reports — perhaps called school or school district report cards — on school performance?

- Does the state fund specific programs (if so, which ones) or do schools just receive general aid?

Having a handle on what school personnel are required to do allows you to better understand the pressures on them, so you don't ask for more than they are able to give. It also allows you to focus on the proper authorities when you are seeking some kind of change. Your hypothetical committee, for instance, may decide to recommend reducing special education costs by placing more handicapped students in regular classrooms (what educators refer to as "mainstreaming" them). You'll just be wasting your breath, though, if your state's laws forbid such a move or if your plan will have to be negotiated with the teachers' union.

How do you find out about state rules and regulations? A telephone call to your state department of education should provide you with the information you want or, at least, guidance on how to find it. You may need to be persistent if your initial effort doesn't get you to the person or the information you want. In most states, the state school boards association, state Parent Teacher Association (PTA), or League of Women Voters will also be able to help you. These organizations usually have offices in state capitals.

Local Policies and Practices

It is one thing for laws and regulations to be enacted on a state level and quite another for them to be carried out locally. Going back to our earlier example, you may find the regulations that the district said were state-mandated are really your district's interpretation of state intent (most likely debatable). If so, you and your committee can focus your energies on the local level.

The place to begin is with district policy. What policies have guided or influenced the district's approach to remediation and special education? The answer might be in your district's policy manual. Each school board should have a manual that specifies how state laws and regulations, as well as local policies, are to be implemented in the district. Don't be surprised, however, if you find your district's manual woefully out of date. Ask administrators or school board members how current the policy manual is and where there are significant deviations between written policies and actual practice.

In some states, a great deal of latitude is given to local districts; in others, the state maintains tighter control over education decisions and how they are implemented. Obviously, knowledge of local policies is more important in the former than in the latter. But regardless of where the regulations are promulgated, you might have occasion to want information on such policies and practices as:

- How staff are evaluated and what procedures exist for getting rid of incompetent personnel.
- How staff are eliminated when there is a reduction in the work force. Can senior staff "bump" those with less time in the system even if they have never taught a particular subject?
- Which local, as well as state, standardized tests are used in the district.
- How changes in curriculum, new courses of study, and selection of textbooks are handled in the district. Is there, for instance, any parent/citizen involvement?
- How school and district policies are established. Do individual schools have school-site councils made up of parents, citizens, and school personnel? If so, what authority do they have? Is there a similar, district-wide council or some sort of district advisory committee to provide input to the board of education?

You won't need to know everything at once, of course, and over time you are likely to learn more and more about your schools, but if you do need information there are organizations and individuals in your neighborhood that can help you. Depending on the information you are seeking, you might contact:

Parent-Teacher Associations (PTAs) — in some communities known as Parent-Teacher Organizations (PTOs) or Home and School Associations. These groups are made up of informed parents, teachers, and community members (often parents who no longer have children in the school but are still interested in it) who know the issues facing their schools and districts, especially where schools need improvement. Call the school principal's office for the name and number of the organization's president.

School district central office personnel. The number of professional staff in a district varies with the size of the district. At minimum, there will be a superintendent of schools (who may, in one- and two-school districts, also be a school principal) and, usually, an assistant superintendent for business or a board secretary who is responsible for gathering and monitoring budget and appropriations information. Larger districts may also have one or more assistant superintendents, a director of curriculum, and supervisors or coordinators for special subject areas, such as reading, math, and special education. There may also be a transportation coordinator, a buildings and grounds supervisor, and a purchasing agent. If you call the district office, the receptionist or secretary who answers can give you the names and titles of the professionals that work there. Face-to-face or telephone interviews with them can yield a great deal of information about such things as average class size; teacher salaries as compared to districts of similar size; the condition of school buildings and any renovation or building plans; teacher-student ratios; state and local test results; and curriculum-strengthening efforts.

Current and former school board members. These people can give you information on the local political climate as it affects schools, and insight into strengths and weaknesses of the school system over time. Better talk to more than one though, to get a more balanced picture. You can probably get some names and addresses from the district's central office. If not, ask at your library.

Teacher association or union officials. Again, your school district office should be able to give you the name of the president of the local professional association or union. He or she will give you insight into the school system's strengths and weaknesses from the perspective of the teaching staff.

Special education parents groups. If there are such groups in your community, ask their leaders for information about special education programs in the district and parents' perspectives on their strengths and weaknesses. The district office should be able to provide you with names, since special education groups usually try to stay in close communication with school authorities. If you come up dry there, try calling individual schools.

Your approach to gathering information from school authorities will be critical to getting essential information on the school district. Their degree of candor will depend on how threatened they feel. If they believe your only interest is in helping the schools, as opposed to leading a crusade to put them under fire, they are more likely to speak openly with you. The tact with which you present yourself and your interests will determine your success. Of course, if the political situation in your district's schools is hot and school personnel feel under attack, you may not be able to reach many of these people at all. In such a case, you will have to depend on written, public information about the schools, on parent groups, and on what you can learn by attending meetings and hearings.

Test Results

One important source of information is test results. Most states now require some form of state-wide testing in addition to tests given at the discretion of teachers, schools, and school districts. These tests are typically one of two kinds — criterion-referenced or norm-referenced.

Criterion-referenced tests are designed to measure the skills and knowledge students have acquired in one or more subject areas. Scores are reported in terms of how well students did in comparison to a performance standard. Minimum competency tests are a form of criterion-referenced test designed to determine whether a student has gained the skills and knowledge judged necessary to go on to a higher grade or to meet the minimum demands of adult life. They are typically administered at several grade levels and, in some states, are required for obtaining a high-school diploma.

Norm-referenced tests compare individual students to a norm group — a group of students of the same age or grade who already took the test. Norms are usually based on national samples. These standardized tests are used to judge how well students in a given class, grade, school, or school district are doing in relation to other students nationally. Some commonly used norm-referenced tests are the Stanford Achievement Test, the Scholastic Aptitude Test (SAT), and the Comprehensive Test of Basic Skills (CTBS).

There is disagreement about the impact of testing. Research on effective schools demonstrates that tests administered to assess whether or not students have learned what was taught are a useful tool — but only when results are used to make appropriate changes to instruction.

However, state-wide tests used to assess not only individual student progress, but also how well schools and school districts are doing their jobs, produce a very different result; they tend to drive curriculum. If a state test given to third graders in the middle of the school year contains questions or problems related to a math concept taught later, students in those schools will not do as well as others in the state who were taught the concept earlier. The school district, not wanting to look bad, will respond by changing its curriculum to meet the test. Whether this influence over curriculum is good or bad depends on how good the tests are, but it is important to realize that standardized tests tend to produce a standardized curriculum and to erode local control over the content, scope, and sequence of what is being taught. This holds true for any standardized test, especially if results are released to the public. If you are seeking curricular changes in your district, you will have to keep this dynamic in mind.

Test results are generally reported to the public by grade level, either school-by-school or for the district as a whole. These scores can indicate a school's strengths and provide some clues to areas for improvement. For instance, if sixth graders are consistently scoring below national norms in math but not in reading, the math program probably needs changing. Perhaps the topics covered in the test are not being taught until later, as discussed above, or maybe they aren't being covered in sufficient depth. When the results are further broken down by sex or race or other subgroups, specific instances where schools are failing their students can be pinpointed. If certain groups of students — children from disadvantaged families, for instance — are consistently scoring lower than other students, school personnel will have to take a hard look at how they are teaching those children and the expectations they have of them.

Here are some questions you might want to ask about test scores in your school:

- How does this year's performance compare to last year's? The year before that? A difference of a few points either way means little, but a consistent increase or decline over time can be meaningful. If there has been a decline, you might want to find out why. Perhaps the students are different — more from disadvantaged homes, for instance — and the program has not been changed to meet their needs. Perhaps the curriculum has been altered so that it no longer conforms to the test.

- What percentage of your students scored at the very bottom or at the very top of the standardized tests given in your school? When the data are organized by gender, ethnicity, or family income level, do the percentages at the top and bottom change significantly from group to group?

- What percentage of your high-school students took the Scholastic Aptitude Test (SAT) last year? What percentage of them scored between 200-299, 300-399, 400-499, 500-599, 600-699, and 700-799 in math and in verbal skills? How does this compare with previous years? With other schools with approximately the same percentage of students taking the test? If another college entrance exam is commonly used in your community, its results can be similarly analyzed.

Be cautious about too much emphasis on test results, however. A study by the National Science Foundation showed that the most common types of question used on standardized tests encourage superficial learning of easily forgotten information instead of problem-solving and critical thinking.[30] Pressure for a school to do well in such tests can lead to an emphasis on drill and practice, which not only takes time from higher-order skill development, but also leads to bored, disinterested students. Test results are only one measure of school quality.

School Budgets

Your school district's budget is a useful source of information when you are trying to make judgments about particular programs or about the district as a whole. Underfunded schools and school programs are often unsuccessful. Yet school districts must operate within financial limitations. If yours is a district where budgets are voted upon, you will want to be sure your tax dollars are being used well, and for the programs you think are most important, before you cast your ballot. And your hypothetical committee will want to review the budget to see how funds are allocated to remedial and special education and where cuts causing the least harm might be made. In either case, it will help to know how budgets are put together.

School districts receive the bulk of their revenues through local, state, and federal taxes. They may also receive small amounts from fees (such as payments for lunches and admissions to sporting events), tuition from out-of-district students, and donations from businesses. The largest source of revenue for most districts is local taxes, although some poor districts receive the biggest proportion of their monies from state revenues.

State support is apportioned according to a formula based on need, the number of pupils, or both. Some support comes with restrictions on how it may be spent. South Carolina, for example, requires some of its state aid be used to maintain an average class size of no more than 20 students in reading and math in grades one through three. New Jersey allocates a portion of its aid to programs for at-risk students.

Federal support for education has been reduced significantly in the past few years, but districts still receive monies for compensatory education, bilingual education, and other special programs through federal block grants to the state, while U.S. Department of Agriculture reimbursements help offset the costs of providing lunches to students.

School district funds are typically expended in six general cate-gories:

- General Operations — expenses for the regular, daily operation of schools, such as salaries for classroom teachers, administrators, and custodians; instructional materials and equipment; heating fuel; and electricity.

- Special Programs — expenses for the operation of programs or specific projects, such as compensatory, bilingual, and special education programs, where monies must be accounted for separately.

- Food Services — expenses from the operation of breakfast and lunch programs.

- Capital Improvements — expenses for the construction of new buildings or the addition to or remodeling of existing buildings.

- Debt Service — the interest and principal on long-term debt, such as the loans taken or bonds sold to build new schools.

- Pupil Activities — expenses for extracurricular activities, such as sports programs.

The largest percentage of your district's budget is consumed by the first category — General Operations. This section of the budget is divided into several functions or services. Each function is assigned a number. While the categories and numbering system may vary somewhat from what is described below, your district's budget will probably be divided something like this:

Code	Function or Service
1000	Instructional Programs
	1100 General
	1200 Special Education
	1300 Adult/Continuing Education
2000	Support Services
	2100 Pupil
	2200 Instructional Staff
	2300 General Administration
	2400 Finance and Operations
2500	Operation and Maintenance of Plant
2600	Pupil Transportation

Each function or service is divided again into more specific parts. For example, General Instructional Programs can have four or five major subcategories such as:

    1100   General Instruction
                1110 Pre-School Programs (Kindergarten)
                1120 Primary Programs
                1130 Elementary Programs (Middle/Junior High)
                1140 High-School Programs
                1150 Vocational Programs

Each of these subcategories is further broken down into such line items as teacher salaries, substitute teacher stipends, instructional supplies, and phone charges. While you as an individual may have little need or desire to get down to this level of budgeting, your committee charged with making recommendations about cost savings will certainly want to.

Your committee will also want to review audit reports (which show actual expenditures) from previous years. Just looking at one number won't provide much information; you need to compare figures over time. You might want to ask district administrators to provide you with:

- the percentage of total school monies that was allocated or expended in a particular function or code during a given year;
- the history of expenditures in that function or code over a period of years;
- the percentage increase or decrease from last year to this year;
- the percentage that actual expenditures are over or under allocated amounts;
- the percentage of the total revenues in a category coming from each major source of revenue each year for the past several years;
- the percentage increase or decrease in each source of revenue over the years.

Since school budgets fluctuate from year to year, it is easier and more revealing to compare percentages rather than dollars. For instance, you might feel pretty satisfied to find that your district's spending on instruction increased from $8,000,000 in 1989 to

$10,500,000 in 1992. But these figures might mask a problem that should concern you. Suppose that, during the same period, the total budget rose from 10 million to 15 million dollars. This would mean that the percentage of total expenditures allocated to instruction actually fell from 80 to 70 percent, a disturbing trend. The percentage decrease, rather than the increase in dollars, is your warning signal that the district's priorities have changed.

You can get information about your district's budget in several ways. You can review it when it is presented to the public at formal hearings, or you can sit in on budget preparation meetings (they should be open to the public). The advantage of doing this is that you can ask questions and make suggestions before a new budget is settled on. If you favor retention of French classes that the board seems bent on eliminating, for example, you might ask about the impact on students who have started and will not be able to continue French, and you can present statistics about language offerings in similar districts. Before the budget is put to public vote, the district may distribute a pamphlet or brochure describing its spending plans for the next year or it may publish a synopsis of the budget in an ad in local newspapers (doing so may be a state requirement). Local newspapers may also publish articles about proposed allocations, but they are unlikely to go into much detail. Sometimes you'll find enlightening letters to the editor attacking or defending particular budget proposals. All these sources can be helpful in making up your mind whether to vote yes or no on a particular budget package, but if you really need to analyze the contents, you'll have to grit your teeth and look at a copy of the full budget. You'll find one at your board of education office and, maybe, at your local school and public library as well. Previous years' budgets should be availalbe at the same locations.

If your favorite school program is eliminated for financial reasons, don't give up. This book has shown that there are strategies you can employ to get the kinds of schools you want. You can become a citizen gadfly and lobby the school board to restore the program; you can rally the public on behalf of your cause; you can campaign for school board members who support your views; you can run for the board yourself; or you can lead or join efforts to raise money for the program in the private sector.

How Your School and District Measure Up to Others

In some cases, you may acquire information about your school or school district, but not be able to draw conclusions from it. What are you to make of your district's average SAT score of 504, dropout rate of 20 percent, student-teacher ratio of 16 to 1, or annual spending of $6,780 per pupil?

The best way to make sense out of most of this data is to compare your school or district with others like it. If your schools are coming up short, you may have reason to be unhappy. And you may be able to use the information to rally your community to seek improvement. Be warned, though. Good comparative data is often hard to find, partly because it is difficult to collect and partly because those who fear embarrassment tend to keep information under wraps.

In some communities, comparisons are easier because of the availability of school report cards, public documents designed to inform citizens about each school in their community or about their school district as a whole. There are two likely sources for report cards on your schools: the school district and the state. Some locally produced report cards are of low quality, bland reports that trumpet success and mask failure. But an increasing number of districts are producing valuable documents that allow educators and the community to evaluate progress toward educational objectives. Some states produce report cards for all districts or all schools. The uniformity of these reports facilitates comparison, but prohibits inclusion of data relating to local goals and objectives. California has adopted a hybrid report card format, in which the state stipulates data that report cards must contain, but allows leeway for local additions.

So call your school or district administrative office to find out if your school has a report card. If it does, ask for reports from previous years, too, so you can see if it is making progress. And if similar schools in your district or similar schools in other districts use the same format, you may wish to call their offices to request copies so you can compare results. You don't know which schools are similar to yours? You may be able to get advice from your district office, a county office, the state department of education, or the state school boards association.

But suppose you study your school report card and find it is uninformative, incomplete, or hard to interpret. Or that it has little relationship to the school's improvement plan. Sure, you can just throw it out. Or you can decide that your commitment to education will be to campaign for an improved version. It's an ambitious task and you may need to recruit allies — such as a parents organization (see pages 53-55) or a local education foundation (see pages 90-110) — to accomplish your aim. For ideas about how to proceed, see the National Education Goals Panel publication, *Handbook for Local Goals Reports* (see Reading List).

If neither your state nor your district publishes school report cards, you still may be able to gather comparison data by contacting your state department of education, state school boards association, state teachers union, or state administrators association. In some states, these organizations provide comparisons of expenditure per pupil for various line items, teacher salaries and benefits, graduation requirements, test results, and other data.

Another, more time-consuming route, is to seek data that interests you from a few other school districts and perform comparisons of your own. Choose districts that are most like yours in terms of size, number of schools, and socio-economic characteristics. You may find the process unworkable if the districts collect different data or report it in incompatible formats.

In any effort to compare schools, remember that haphazard or inappropriate comparisons can be very misleading because of differing background conditions — the impact of decaying neighborhoods, the number of special education students, and the like. Don't assume your school or district is derelict, and certainly don't "go public" with your conclusions until you give administrators an opportunity to explain the comparative data that makes them look bad.

Remember, too, that some of the most important things about schools — the attitude of teachers, an atmosphere of order and purpose, a spirit of inquiry, a love of learning, a sense of collegiality, a drive to see that all students succeed — cannot be put into numbers. The only way to compare schools on these qualities is to visit them and form your own, unquantifiable opinion.

Section Four: RESOURCES

This section contains lists of organizations, federal agencies, clearinghouses, books and periodicals that can provide you with information and advice about helping public schools. It also contains a glossary of educational terminology, so that you can more easily understand educational professionals and be more professional yourself when dealing with them.

The first list is of organizations that might be useful in your efforts to help your public schools. If you're not sure whether an organization shares your interests, you can usually get a good idea of where it stands by scanning a copy of its publication list.

Associations and Other Non-Profit Organizations

ASPIRA Association, Inc.
1112 16th Street NW, Suite 340
Washington, DC 20036
202/835-3600
Contact: Lisa Colon

> ASPIRA is a national **Hispanic education leadership development** organization. It administers a national parent involvement demonstration project in Hispanic communities in nine cities and produces booklets to help Hispanic parents with their children's education.

Carnegie Council on Adolescent Development
2400 N Street, NW, 6th Floor
Washington, DC 20037-1153
202/429-7979

> This council was established in 1986 by the Carnegie Corporation to bring attention to **the needs of adolescents**. Its Task Force on Education of Young Adolescents has looked at new approaches to foster adolescent development and education. The report of that task force, *Turning Points*, highlights the need for new and stronger connections among schools, families, and community agencies.

Center for Civic Education
5146 Douglas Fir Road
Calabasas, CA 91302
Contact: Charles Quigley

The Center for Civic Education is developing proposed **national standards for education in civics,** due in summer 1994.

Center for Excellence in Education: See *National Alliance of Business*

Center for the Study of Reading
174 Children's Research Center
51 Gerty Drive
Champaign, IL 61820
Contact: Jean Osborn

The Center for the Study of Reading is developing proposed **national standards for education in reading,** due in fall 1995.

Center on Families, Communities, Schools and Children's Learning: See *School and Family Connections Project*

Children's Defense Fund (CDF)
25 E Street, NW
Washington, DC 20001
202/628-8787

CDF is an **advocacy organization for children,** especially those who are handicapped or from poor and minority families. It seeks to educate the nation about the needs of children and the importance of taking preventative measures before they get sick, drop out of school, or get into trouble. CDF gathers and disseminates information and, through its network of state and local child advocates, lobbies state and national governments on behalf of children's welfare.

Cities In Schools (CIS)
401 Wythe Street, Suite 200
Alexandria, VA 22314
703/519-8999
Contact: Bonnie Nance Frazier

CIS is a national organization dedicated to **dropout prevention** in cities and communities of all sizes. It operates by bringing together existing public and private resources and helping them focus their attention on schools, where they concentrate on at-risk students. Typically, a local CIS program forms a team of social workers, employment counselors, educators, health professionals, volunteers, and mentors to work with students. CIS offers free, multi-day training courses at Lehigh University in Bethlehem, PA, for people interested in establishing a Cities In Schools program (trainees are responsible for their own transportation, room, and board); it also offers training in its regional centers in Los Angeles, Chicago, Atlanta, Austin, TX, and Mars, PA, near Pittsburgh. Callers can receive free training materials, information packets, and details about volunteering at one of CIS's current sites or about establishing a new project.

Coalition of Essential Schools
Brown University
Box 1969
Providence, RI 02912
401/863-2847

> The Coalition, founded by Brown University Professor Theodore Sizer, promotes **secondary school reform**, with emphasis on pedagogy, curriculum assessment, and community support. The coalition can advise callers how to visit one of 500 affiliated public schools.

Council for Educational Development and Research (CEDR)
1825 I Street, NW #400
Washington, DC 20006
202/429-5533
Contact: Judy Damiani

> CEDR members are education **research** and development institutions that create programs and materials, including publications on parent involvement, useful for educators, parents, and others interested in the public schools.

Council for Exceptional Children: See *ERIC Clearinghouse on Handicapped and Gifted Children* (p. 192)

Council for the Advancement and Support of Education (CASE)
11 Dupont Circle, Suite 400
Washington, DC 20036
202/328-5900

> While dedicated primarily to post-secondary education, CASE can be helpful to anyone interested in providing **matching gifts**

to K-12 schools. CASE's annual publication, *Matching Gift Details,* describes current matching gift programs of participating companies, including many that match gifts to public elementary and secondary schools. CASE's National Clearinghouse for Corporate Matching Gift Information sends pamphlets and provides advice to employers interested in starting new matching gift programs.

Education Commission of the States (ECS)
707 17th Street, Suite 2700
Denver, CO 80202-3427
303/299-3600

ECS is a non-profit, **interstate compact** formed in 1965 to help governors, state legislators, state education officials, and others develop policies to improve the quality of education at all levels. ECS is involved in a joint effort (Re:Learning) with the Coalition of Essential Schools to stimulate and support the redesign of the public education system. Information available from ECS includes publications on restructuring the education system.

Home and School Institute, Inc. (HSI)
1500 Massachusetts Avenue, N.W. #42
Washington, DC 20005
202/466-3633
Contact: Dorothy Rich

HSI conducts demonstration projects, training programs, and conferences designed to improve the quality of education by **integrating the resources of the home, school, and community.** It designs and conducts practical self-help programs, with special emphasis on materials to be used at home by parents and their children. Its MegaSkills workshops, for school personnel, parents, and citizens, are conducted throughout the country.

I Have a Dream Foundation (IHAD)
330 7th Avenue, 20th Floor
New York, NY 10001
212/736-1730

The national IHAD Foundation seeks to expand the number of local I Have A Dream projects (for a description of such projects, see pages 83-85), develops policy and monitoring procedures for them, and helps them organize and adapt to local circumstances.

It also works to expand private and public sources for project and program support, and tests and promotes modifications and adaptations of IHAD project structures and content. The Foundation can provide callers with information about IHAD programs and about volunteer opportunities in local IHAD projects.

Institute for Responsive Education (IRE)
605 Commonwealth Avenue
Boston, MA 02215
617/353-3309
Contact: Owen Heleen

This national research and advocacy organization studies, promotes, and assists **citizen participation** in educational decision-making and helps schools become more responsive to citizen and parent concerns. Affiliated with the School of Education at Boston University, IRE publishes the journal *Equity and Choice* and various reports, and is the principal contact for the new National Center on Families.

International Reading Association (IRA)
800 Barksdale Road
Newark, DE 19711-3269
302/731-1600

IRA works with parents, educators, and researchers to improve **reading instruction** and increase literacy.

Mexican American Legal Defense and Educational Fund (MALDEF)
634 South Spring Street, 11th Floor
Los Angeles, CA 90014
213/629-2512
Contact: Luisa Perez-Ortega

MALDEF is a civil rights organization that conducts a Parent Leadership Program for promoting the **participation of Latino parents as leaders at their children's schools**. The program involves a 12-week course, including parent-teacher conferences and meetings with school-district officials.

Music Educators National Conference
1902 Association Drive
Reston, VA 22091
Contact: John Mahlmann

The Music Educators National Conference is developing **national standards for arts** education, due in summer 1994.

National Academy of Sciences
2101 Constitution Avenue
Washington, DC 20418
Contact: Ken Hoffman

The National Academy of Sciences is developing **national standards for science** education, due in summer 1994.

National Alliance of Business (NAB)
Center for Excellence in Education
1201 New York Avenue, NW, Suite 700
Washington, DC 20005
202/289-2925

The Center promotes and supports **business involvement** in educational restructuring, bringing together business, government, education, and community organizations in efforts to foster fundamental change throughout the educational system. NAB's annual Business/Education Forum is an important venue for information exchange and networking among leaders in the business, education, and non-profit communities.

National Association of Partners in Education (NAPE)
209 Madison Street, Suite 401
Alexandria, VA 22314
703/836-4880

NAPE is a membership organization dedicated to encouraging and improving **partnerships** of schools, businesses, community groups, educators, and individual volunteers to help students achieve educational excellence. NAPE sells a wide variety of helpful publications, such as *Creating and Managing a Business/Education Partnership*; *How to Organize and Manage School Volunteer Programs*; *Organizing Effective School-Based Mentoring Programs*; and *Creating and Managing Effective School Site Councils/Shared Decision Making*. It also sells and rents videos, and holds an annual symposium that can be valuable for those who want to learn about the variety of partnerships and about how to improve and expand collaborative efforts. The symposium is also valuable for the opportunity it gives attendees to network among leaders in education, business, and social services. An important component of NAPE is the National School Volunteer Program, a coalition of volunteers in education.

National Black Child Development Institute
1023 15th Street, N.W. #600
Washington, DC 20005
202/387-1281
Contact: Sherry Deane

The National Black Child Development Institute provides direct services and conducts advocacy campaigns to improve the quality of life for **black children and youth**. Family and early childhood education are emphasized, and speakers and publications are available.

National Center for History in the Schools
231 Moore Hall 405 Hilgard Avenue
Los Angeles, CA 90024
310/825-4702
Contact: Charlotte Crabtree

The National Center for History in the Schools is developing **national standards for the teaching of history**, due in spring 1994.

National Center on Families: See *Institute for Responsive Education*

National Clearinghouse for Corporate Matching Gift Information: See *Council for the Advancement and Support of Education*

National Coalition for Parent Involvement in Education (NCPIE)
Box 39
Washington, DC 20036

This organization is composed of more than 30 national education and community life associations that collaborate in their efforts to encourage and increase involvement in public schools. It is dedicated to developing effective **family and school partnerships**. If you are unsure about where to turn, it can direct inquiries to appropriate member organizations.

National Coalition of Advocates for Students (NCAS)
100 Boylston Street, Suite 737
Boston, MA 02116
617/357-9549

> The NCAS is a **coalition of state advocacy organizations,** education law centers, and such national organizations as the Children's Defense Fund, the National Council of La Raza, and the National Black Child Development Institute. NCAS offers a wide range of publications, and sells them at a discount to its "subscribers." It also offers free newsletters on its school reform concepts and on immigrant education.

National Committee for Citizens in Education (NCCE)
900 Second Street, NE, Suite 8
Washington, DC 20002
800-NETWORK

> NCCE promotes local action to improve the quality of education and acts as an advocate for **parent and citizen involvement** in schools. It offers numerous publications and a hot-line (using an on-line database) to provide information to parents and other citizens about public schools and how to be more effective in dealing with them. Its numerous, jargon-free publications include an informative newsletter, *Network for Public Schools*, handbooks on many topics, and books and manuals on how parents and citizens can become involved in education decisions at the local level.

National Community Education Association (NCEA)
801 North Fairfax Street #209
Alexandria, VA 22314
703/683-NCEA

> NCEA's purpose is to support and advance **parent and community involvement** in elementary and secondary education, interagency cooperation to address community needs, and learning opportunities in the community for residents of all ages and educational backgrounds. It hosts an annual conference and publishes a monthly newsletter, quarterly journal, and occasional handbooks on community education-related topics.

National Council of Geographic Education
Geography Standards Project
1600 M Street, NW
Washington, DC 20036
Contact: Anthony DeSouza

The National Council of Geographic Education is preparing **national standards for geography** education, due in winter 1993.

National Council of La Raza (NCLR)
810 First Street, NE, Suite 300
Washington, DC 20002-4205
202/289-1380
Contact: Denise De La Roas

NCLR is a **research and advocacy** organization that works on behalf of the U.S. **Hispanic** population and provides technical assistance to community-based organizations. It publishes materials on migrant, bilingual, and general education issues, many of which treat the issue of parent and community involvement in schools. NCLR's Project EXCEL is a national education demonstration project that includes tutoring services and parent education.

National Council of Teachers of Mathematics (NCTM)
1906 Association Drive
Reston, VA 22091

The NCTM has developed **national standards for education in mathematics**. Published as *Curriculum and Evaluation Standards for Mathematics*, the standards may be purchased for $25 by writing to NCTM's Order Processing Department.

National Dropout Prevention Center (NDPC)
Clemson University
P.O. Box 345111
Clemson, SC 29634-5111
803/656-0136
Contact: Maraquita Presley

NDPC has a national database of **dropout prevention** programs and can provide callers with information about their components, their funding, and their locations. Dropout programs can register as members and receive a newsletter and other benefits.

National Education Association (NEA)
1201 16th Street, NW
Washington, DC 20036
202/833-4000

> The largest **teachers union** in the country, NEA has an extensive collection of books, pamphlets, and videos about the teaching profession, problems in education, and such issues as adolescent suicide, homeless students, teacher burnout, school violence, and student pregnancy. NEA also publishes the annual *Rankings of the States*, a valuable comparison of data about enrollments, faculty, and financial issues in all 50 states.

National Information Center for Children and Youth with Handicaps (NICCYH)
P.O. Box 1492
Washington, DC 20013-1492
800/999-5599

> NICCYH provides free information to assist parents, educators, caregivers, advocates, and others interested in helping **children and youth with disabilities**. It provides information on local, state, and national disability groups, and maintains databases with current information on disability topics. Publications include *News Digest* and *Parent Guides.*

National Mentoring Working Group
One to One Partnership
2801 M Street, NW
Washington, DC 20037
202/338-3844
Contact: Susan Mason

> The National Mentoring Working Group acts as a catalyst in mobilizing networks of people and communities to meet the needs of at-risk youth, supports existing **mentoring** efforts, and encourages the establishment of new ones. Materials available from the Group include a list of publications about mentoring and how to set up mentoring programs, a fact sheet on the National Mentoring Initiative, and a pamphlet on the elements of effective mentoring practices.

National Parent-Teacher Association (PTA)
700 North Rush Street
Chicago, IL 60611-2571
312/787-0977

> The national PTA is the largest education **volunteer association** in the country. You do not have to have children, school-age or otherwise, to be a member. For a free list of its publications, send a stamped, self-addressed, business-sized envelope to Publications List, National PTA, Department D at the above address. Local PTAs may also have the list.

National School Boards Association (NSBA)
1680 Duke Street
Alexandria, VA 22314
703/838-6722

> NSBA is a **federation of state school boards associations**. It provides information on such topics as curriculum development, and legislation and court decisions affecting education and school policy. You can get the address and telephone number of your state school boards association by calling the NSBA.

National School Volunteer Program: See *National Association of Partners in Education*

One to One: See *National Mentoring Working Group*

Project EXCEL: See *National Council of La Raza*

Public Education Fund Network (PEF/NET)
501 13th Street, NW
Washington, DC 20005-3808
202/628-7460

> PEF/NET is an outgrowth of the Public Education Fund, which, in the mid-1980s, disbursed $6 million in Ford Foundation funds to help develop **local education foundations** (LEFs) in low-income urban communities nationwide. Today, the organization provides training and technical assistance to member LEFs and assists emerging funds. It can help callers by identifying nearby LEFs and by providing copies of its excellent publications about forming LEFs and establishing mini-grant programs for teachers and administrators.

Public Education Institute (PEI)
Building 4090, Livingston Campus
New Brunswick, NJ 08903
908/463-1603
Contact: Herb Green

This New Jersey organization promotes **public involvement** in education, with a number of programs, including its Public Policy and Public Schools course. This course trains citizens in the structure and practices of public schools and how to influence them. PEI provides information on the course to schools and citizen groups throughout the country.

Recruiting New Teachers, Inc. (RNT)
6 Standish Street
Cambridge, MA 02138
800/458-3224

RNT seeks to **encourage people to become teachers** by providing them with extensive information about training, financial aid, certification, and job opportunities, and by operating a clearinghouse for teachers seeking employment.

School and Family Connections Project Center
The Johns Hopkins University
3505 North Charles Street
Baltimore, MD 21218
301/338-7570

The School and Family Connections Project studies and implements **school-family cooperation**. Its publications and other materials may be helpful to administrators, teachers, parents, and citizens.

Teach For America (TFA)
P.O. Box 5114
New York, NY 10185
800/832-1230

Teach for America seeks to **encourage** recent college graduates and older Americans to pursue **teaching careers** in inner cities and in rural areas experiencing teacher shortages. TFA provides training to prepare teachers for these assignments, and helps them find employment. The organization provides information packets to callers.

Federal Agencies

Depending on your specific interest, the following federal agencies may have information you can use. A letter explaining what you are trying to do and the information you need should bring you some form of response, even if it is only to point you in another direction.

Administration for Children, Youth and Families
Office of Human Development Services
Department of Health and Human Services
330 C Street SW
Washington, DC 20201
202/205-8347

Compensatory Education Programs
Office of Elementary and Secondary Education
Department of Education
400 Maryland Avenue, SW
Washington, DC 20202-7240
202/401-1682

Office of Educational Research and Improvement
555 New Jersey Avenue NW
Washington, DC 20208
202/219-2050

Center on Families, Communities, Schools, and Children's Learning
605 Commonwealth Avenue 6th Floor
Boston, MA 02215
617/353-3309

National Research Center on Education in the Inner Cities
Center for Research in Human Development and Education
Ritter Hall Annex 9th Floor
Temple University
Philadelphia, PA 19122
215/787-3001

ERIC Clearinghouses

Supported by the U.S. Department of Education, the Educational Resource Information Center (ERIC) manages the world's largest educational database. ERIC staff can help you find answers to education-related questions, refer you to appropriate information sources, and provide you with relevant publications. Services include providing research summaries, bibliographies, reference and referral services, computer searches, and document reproduction. ERIC staff can also tell you how you, your public library, or your public school can access ERIC databases directly, using a computer and modem. You can then look up, by topic or by author, just about everything that has been published on education in the last twenty years and download information to your computer.

The best way to start is to call the general ERIC number, 800-LET-ERIC, and ask for information about the system. For more specific information, write or call the specialized clearinghouses. The clearinghouses will also put your name on mailing lists for their publications.

ERIC also offers a book and a videotape describing its entire system. The book, which sells for $10, is *A Parent's Guide to the ERIC Database: Where to Turn with Your Questions About Schooling*. The video, which comes with a 90-page manual and costs $35, is *A Workshop About ERIC: The Education Information Resource.*

The Clearinghouses and their specialties are:

- ERIC Clearinghouse on Adult, Career, and Vocational Education, The Ohio State University, 1900 Kenny Road Columbus, OH 43210-1090 800/848-4815

- ERIC Clearinghouse on Counseling and Personnel Services, University of Michigan School of Education, 610 East University Street Room 2108, Ann Arbor, MI 48109-1259 313/764-9492

- ERIC Clearinghouse on Educational Management, University of Oregon, 1787 Agate Street, Eugene, OR 97403-5207 503/346-5043.

- ERIC Clearinghouse on Elementary and Early Childhood Education, University of Illinois College of Education, 805 W. Pennsylvania Avenue, Urbana, IL 61801-4897 217/333-1386.

- ERIC Clearinghouse on Handicapped and Gifted Children, Council for Exceptional Children, 1920 Association Drive, Reston, VA 22091-1589 703/264-9474

- ERIC Clearinghouse on Information Resources, Syracuse University, Huntington Hall Room 030, Syracuse, NY 13244-2340 315/443-3640

- ERIC Clearinghouse on Reading and Communication Skills, Indiana University, Smith Research Center Suite 150, 2805 East 10th Street, Bloomington, IN 47408-2698 800/759-4723

- ERIC Clearinghouse on Rural Education and Small Schools, Appalachia Educational Laboratory, 1031 Quarrier Street, P. O. Box 1348, Charleston, WV 25325-1348 800/624-9120.

- ERIC Clearinghouse on Science, Mathematics, and Environmental Education, The Ohio State University, 1200 Chambers Road Room 310, Columbus, OH 43212-1792 614/292-6717

- ERIC Clearinghouse on Social Studies/Social Science Education, Indiana University, Social Studies Development Center, 2805 East 10th Street Suite 120, Bloomington, IN 47408-2698 812/855-3838

- ERIC Clearinghouse on Teacher Education, American Association of Colleges for Teacher Education, One Dupont Circle, NW Suite 610, Washington, DC 20036-2412 202/293-2450

- ERIC Clearinghouse on Tests, Measurement, and Evaluation, American Institutes for Research, Washington Research Center, 3333 K Street, NW, Washington, DC 20007-3541 202/342-5060

- ERIC Clearinghouse on Urban Education, Teachers College, Columbia University, Box 40, New York, NY 10027-9998 212/678-3433.

- Adjunct ERIC Clearinghouse for Art Education, Indiana University, Social Studies Development Center, 2805 East 10th Street Suite 120, Bloomington, IN 47408-2698 812/855-3838

Reading List

You may find these publications useful in understanding the public schools, problems in education, proposed solutions, and how you can become involved.

Adams, Don and Paul Snodgrass, eds. *A Manager's Handbook to Partnerships: How to Set-Up, Run and Maintain Partnerships.* Ellenton, FL: InfoMedia, 1990.

An Advocate's Guide to Improving Education. Washington, D.C.: Children's Defense Fund, 1990.

Atkinson, Carroll, and Maleska, Eugene T. *The Story of Education.* Philadelphia and New York: Chilton Books, 1965.

Augenblick, John; Fulton, Mary; and Pipho, Chris. *School Finance: A Primer.* Denver: Education Commission of the States, 1991.

Augenblick, John; Gold, Steven D.; and McGuire, Kent. *Education Finance in the 1990s.* Denver: Education Commission of the States, 1990.

Becoming a School Partner: A Guide for Older Volunteers. Washington, D.C.: American Association of Retired Persons, 1989.

Berla, Nancy, and Hall, Susan Hlesciak. *Beyond the Open Door: A Citizens Guide to Increasing Public Access to Local School Boards.* Washington, D.C.: The National Committee for Citizens in Education, 1989.

Bloom, Jill. *Parenting Our Schools: A Hands-On Guide to Education Reform.* Boston: Little Brown and Co., 1992.

Brown, Martha C. *Schoolwise: A Parent's Guide to Getting the Best Education for Your Child.* Los Angeles: Jeremy P. Tarcher, 1985.

Business and the Schools: A Guide to Effective Programs. 2nd ed., New York: Council for Aid to Education, 1992.

The Business Leader's Guide to Partnerships for Education Reform. Philadelphia: Public/Private Ventures, 1993.

The Business Roundtable Participation Guide: A Primer for Business on Education. Washington: The National Alliance of Business, 1991.

Committee for Economic Development. *Children in Need: Investment Strategies for the Educationally Disadvantaged.* New York: Committee for Economic Development, 1987

_____. *Investing in Our Children: Business and the Public Schools.* New York: Committee for Economic Development, 1985.

Coons, Christopher, A., and Petrick, Elizabeth W. "A Decade of Making Dreams into Reality: Lessons from the I Have A Dream Program." *Yale Law and Policy Review* xxx (1992): 82-103

Corcoran, Thomas G.; Walker, Lisa J.; White, J. Lynne. *Working in Urban Schools.* Washington, D.C.: Institute for Educational Leadership, 1988.

Cremin, Lawrence A. *Popular Education and Its Discontents.* New York: Harper and Row, 1990.

Criteria for Evaluating an AIDS Curriculum. Boston: National Coalition of Advocates for Students, 1992 (revised).

Cutlip, Glen W., and Shockley, Robert J. *Careers in Teaching.* New York: Rosen Publishing Group, 1988.

Davies, Don, ed. *Schools Where Parents Make a Difference.* Boston: Institute for Responsible Education, 1976.

Dersh, Rhonda E. *The School Budget: It's Your Money, It's Your Business.* Columbia, MD: National Committee for Citizens in Education, 1979.

Education Partnerships in Public Elementary and Secondary Schools. Washington, D.C.: National Center for Education Statistics, 1989.

Strategies for Dropout Prevention. Clemson, SC: National Dropout Prevention Center, 1990.

The Essential Components of a Successful Education System: Putting Policy into Practice. Washington, D.C.: The Business Roundtable, 1992.

Evans, Angela. *Starting Smart: Choosing an Appropriate Partnership with Schools.* Washington, D.C.: National Planning Association, 1990.

Falling By the Wayside: Children in Rural America. Washington, D.C.: Children's Defense Fund, 1992.

Fiske, Edward B. *Smart Schools, Smart Kids: Why Do Some Schools Work?* New York: Simon & Schuster, 1991.

Freedman, Marc. *The Kindness of Strangers: Reflections on the Mentoring Movement.* Philadelphia: Public/Private Ventures, 1992.

Fruchter, Norman. *New Directions for Parent Involvement.* Washington, D.C.: Academy for Educational Development, 1993.

Gardner, Arlene L., ed. *School Partnerships: A Handbook for School and Community Leaders.* New Brunswick, NJ: Public Responsibility for Educational Success, 1990.

The Good Common School: Making the Vision Work for All Children. Boston: National Coalition of Advocates for Students, 1991.

Goodlad, John I. *A Place Called School: Prospect for the Future.* New York: McGraw Hill, 1984.

Gross, Theodore L. *Partners in Education: How Colleges Can Work With Schools to Improve Teaching and Learning.* San Francisco: Jossey-Bass, 1988.

Handbook for Local Goals Reports: Building a Community of Learners; A Handbook for Communities to Develop Local Goals Reports to Measure Their Progress Toward the National Education Goals. Washington, D.C.: National Education Goals Panel, 1993.

Hansen, Barbara J. *School Improvement Councils: A Guide to Effectiveness.* Columbia, SC: School Council Assistance Project, College of Education, University of So. Carolina, 1989.

Hansen, Barbara J., and Marburger, Carl L. *School Based Improvement: A Manual for Training School Councils.* Washington, DC: National Committee for Citizens in Education, 1989.

Harwood Group. *Citizens and Politics: A View from Main Street America.* The Kettering Foundation, 1991.

Henderson, Anne T. *The Evidence Continues to Grow: Parent Involvement Improves Student Achievement.* Columbia, MD: National Committee for Citizens in Education, 1987.

Henderson, Anne T.; Marburger, Carl L. ; and Ooms, Theodora. *Beyond the Bake Sale: An Educator's Guide to Working with Parents.* Columbia, MD: National Committee for Citizens in Education, 1986.

Hodgkinson, Harold L. *All One System: The Demographics of Education.* Washington, D.C.: Institute for Educational Leadership, 1985.

How to Organize an Effective Parent/Advocacy Group and Move Bureaucracies. Chicago: Coordinating Council for Handicapped Children, 1980.

Howley, Craig; Stowers, Phyllis; and Cahape, Patricia. *A Parent's Guide to the ERIC Database: Where to Turn with Your Questions About Schooling.* Charleston, WV: ERIC Clearinghouse on Rural Education and Small Schools, 1992.

Hyman, Carl S., ed. *The School-Community Cookbook: Recipes for Successful Projects in the Schools.* Baltimore: The Fund for Educational Excellence, 1992.

Investing in Our Children: Business and the Public Schools. New York: Committee for Economic Development, 1985.

Kids Count Data Book: State Profiles of Child Well-Being. Washington, D.C.: Center for Social Policy, 1993 (annual).

Kozol, Jonathan. *Savage Inequalities: Children in America's Schools.* New York: Crown Publishers, 1991.

Lacey, Richard A. and Christopher Kingsley. *A Guide to Working Partnerships.* Waltham, MA: Center for Human Resources, 1988.

Lapointe, Archie E.; Mead, Nancy A.; and Askew, Janice M. *Learning Mathematics* and *Learning Science.* Princeton, NJ: Educational Testing Service, 1992.

Levine, Marsha, and Trachtman, Roberta, eds. *American Business and the Public Schools: Case Studies of Corporate Involvement in Public Education.* New York: Teachers College Press, 1988.

Lightfoot, Sarah Lawrence. *Worlds Apart: Relationships Between Families and Schools.* New York: Basic Books, 1978.

Lombana, Judy H. *Home-School Partnerships: Guidelines and Strategies for Educators.* New York: Grune and Stratton, n.d.

Lund, Leonard. *Beyond Business/Education Partnerships: The Business Experience.* New York: The Conference Board, 1988.

Making Sense of School Budgets: A Citizen's Guide to Local Public Education Spending. Washington, D.C.: U.S. Department of Education, 1989.

Marburger, Carl L. *One School at a Time: School-Based Management, A Process for Change.* Columbia, MD: National Committee for Citizens in Education, 1988.

Martz, Larry. *Making Schools Better: How Parents and Teachers Across the Country Are Taking Action — And How You Can, Too.* New York: Times Books, 1992.

Meeting the Challenge: How Communities and Schools Can Improve Education for Immigrant Students. Boston: National Coalition of Advocates for Students, 1993.

The Mentoring Guidebook. Clemson, SC: National Dropout Prevention Center, 1991.

Mentoring Programs for At-Risk Youth. Clemson, SC: National Dropout Prevention Center, 1990.

Moore, Donald, et al. *Standing Up for Children: Effective Child Advocacy in the Schools.* Chicago: Designs for Change, 1989.

National Mentoring Working Group. *Mentoring: Elements of Effective Practice.* The United Way of America, 1991.

Oakes, Jeannie, and Lipton, Martin. *Making the Best of School: A Handbook for Parents, Teachers and Policymakers.* New Haven: Yale University Press, 1990.

Oppenheim, Joanne. *The Elementary School Handbook: Making the Most of Your Child's Education.* New York: Pantheon, 1989.

Otterbourgh, Susan D. *School Partnerships Handbook: How to Set Up and Administer Programs with Business, Government, and Your Community.* Englewood Cliffs, NJ: Prentice-Hall, 1986.

Otterbourgh, Susan D., and Adams, Don. *Partnerships in Educations: Measuring Their Success.* Ellenton, FL: InfoMedia, 1989.

Pizzo, Peggy. *Parent to Parent: How Self-Help and Child Advocacy Groups Can Help You Get Better Schools.* Boston: Beacon Press, 1983.

Powell, Arthur G.; Farrar, Eleanor; and Cohen, David K. *The Shopping Mall High School: Winners and Losers in the Educational Marketplace.* Boston: Houghton Mifflin, 1985.

Ravitch, Diane, and Finn, Chester E., Jr. *What Do Our 17-Year-Olds Know?* New York: Harper and Row, 1987.

Restructuring the Education System: A Consumer's Guide, Volume 1. Denver, CO: Education Commission of the States, 1991.

Rigden, Diana W. *Business/School Partnerships: A Path to Effective School Restructuring.* New York: Council for Aid to Education, 1991.

Schimmel, David, and Fischer, Louis. *Parents, Schools and the Law.* Columbia, MD: National Committee for Citizens in Education, 1987.

School-Community-Business Partnerships: Building Foundations for Dropout Prevention. Clemson, SC: National Dropout Prevention Center, 1990.

School Help: 105 Resources for Chicago School Improvement. Chicago: Designs for Change, 1993.

Schwartz, Cipora O. *How to Run a School Board Campaign and Win.* Washington, D.C.: National Committee for Citizens in Education, n.d.

Sizer, Theodore R. *Horace's Compromise: The Dilemma of the American High School.* Boston: Houghton Mifflin, 1985.

_____. *Horace's School: Redesigning the American High School.* Boston: Houghton Mifflin, 1992.

Slavin, Robert E.; Karweit, Nancy L.; and Madden, Nancy A. *Programs for Students At Risk*. Boston: Allyn and Bacon, 1989.

Sommerfeld, Meg. "Asked to 'Dream,' Students Beat the Odds." *Education Week* (April 8, 1992).

The State of America's Children. Washington, D.C.: Children's Defense Fund, annual.

Thomas, M. Donald. *Your School: How Well Is It Working?* Columbia, MD: National Committee for Citizens in Education, 1982.

Toch, Thomas. *In the Name of Excellence: The Struggle to Reform the Nation's Schools, Why It's Failing, and What Should Be Done*. New York: Oxford University Press, 1991.

Tutoring Success. Clemson, SC: National Dropout Prevention Center, 1991.

The Unfinished Agenda: A New Vision for Child Development and Education. New York: Committee for Economic Development, 1991.

Verstegen, Deborah A. *School Finance At a Glance*. Denver: Education Commission of the States, 1990.

Weinberger, Susan G. *How to Start a Student Mentor Program*. Fastback 333, Phi Delta Kappa, 1992.

Weston, Susan Perkins. *A School Board Budget Primer*. Lexington, KY: Prichard Committee for Academic Excellence, 1992.

Williams, Michael R. *Neighborhood Organizing for Urban School Reform*. New York: Teachers College Press, 1989.

Wirth, Arthur G. *Education and Work for the Year 2000: Choices We Face*. San Francisco: Jossey Bass, 1992.

Wood, George H. *Schools That Work: America's Most Innovative Public Education Programs*. New York: Dutton, 1992.

Your Child's School Records. Washington, D.C.: Children's Defense Fund, 1986.

Zerchykov, Ross. *A Citizen's Notebook for Effective Schools: A Sourcebook of Research Briefs and Local School Improvement Projects*. Boston: Institute for Responsive Education, 1984.

See ERIC Clearinghouses section (p. 190-191) for information on how best to do research on education issues.

Newspapers and Magazines

Education Today is a newsletter published by The Educational Publishing Group, Inc., 376 Boylston Street, Boston, MA 02116. Subscriptions are $14.95/year and can be ordered by calling 800/927-6006. Some corporations, including Merck, TRW, and Bristol-Myers Squibb, subscribe to multiple copies of *Education Today* and distribute them to interested employees. *Education Today* also runs a parent hotline for recorded resource referrals and advice; call 617/446-8321.

Education Week bills itself as "American Education's Newspaper of Record," and that is an accurate description. Published by Editorial Projects in Education, its 40 issues per year contain national, state, and local news; features on problems, reforms, and people; commentary; and book reviews. Subscriptions are $59.94/year and can be ordered by writing to *Education Week*, P.O. Box 2083, Marion, OH 43305.

Phi Delta Kappan is a monthly magazine (except July and August) published by Phi Delta Kappa, P.O. Box 789, Bloomington IN 47402-0789. Phi Delta Kappa is an organization of educators and those interested in education. It also publishes books and pamphlets on education-related topics.

Glossary

Every group has its own jargon. Educators are no different from lawyers, doctors, or plumbers in this regard. Sometimes this vocabulary is used deliberately to keep outsiders in the dark. More often it is used without thinking, just in the course of everyday discussion about work. Whichever the case, if you want to communicate with educators, it will help to know their language. Some words you might hear are:

Ability Grouping: See GROUPING.

Achievement Test: Test given in schools to determine how much a student has learned in a particular subject or in general. Test results may also be used to determine the quality of education being provided.

Accelerated Schools: Schools which place slow learners in accelerated rather than remedial classes, to enable them to catch up to other students in their age group. The chief promoter of this concept is the Accelerated Schools Project, led by Henry M. Levin, professor of education at Stanford University.

Acceleration Programs: Traditionally, an approach to the education of gifted students, which permits them to proceed through an educational program faster than other students their age. In recent years, these programs have also been employed for slow learners; see ACCELERATED SCHOOLS.

Ad Hoc Committee: A committee put together to complete a specific task, and which disbands once its charge has been fulfilled.

Adopt-A-School Program. See SCHOOL-BUSINESS PARTNERSHIP.

Advisory Committee: A committee charged with providing advice to a person (or group, such as a board of education) who has authority to make decisions. The person or group may or may not take the advice of the committee.

Advocacy: Arguing for a cause. Advocacy groups build public support for their point of view in order to influence decision-makers.

Aide: Staff member or volunteer who assists professional educators in classrooms, school libraries, lunchrooms, and playgrounds.

America 2000: A federal government initiative (renamed "Goals 2000" in early 1993) to focus the nation's schools on six national education goals and to create New American Schools. Eleven projects were awarded grants in 1992 (see pages 145-149).

Appropriations: Monies allocated for specific purposes. State legislatures, for instance, appropriate certain funds to be spent on education. Local school districts appropriate funds for textbooks, teacher salaries, etc.

At-Risk Students: Children and youth who are likely, based on their school performance and family situations, to drop out of school, abuse alcohol and drugs, or run afoul of the law.

Basic Skills Test: Test designed to measure students' ability to employ the fundamental skills of reading, writing, and mathematics that are thought to be prerequisites to further learning and achievement. Also see MINIMUM-COMPETENCY TEST.

Bilingual Education: Programs in which students who do not speak English are taught in both English and their native tongues. The goal is to make them proficient in English while keeping up with their age-group in academic studies. These programs sometimes arouse controversy, with opponents claiming that they segregate children or fail to prepare them for mainstream class situations.

Block Grant: Federal funding for education that is distributed in lump sums rather than by categories, permitting greater freedom to states and school districts in determining how the monies are to be spent.

Board of Education: A board of citizens (often referred to as a school board), who are elected or, in three percent of school districts, appointed to oversee local public schools. In some states, the group is known as a board of school trustees or school committee.

Board of School Estimate: A committee, usually made up of municipal and school officials, that determines the amount of tax money to be raised to support the public schools. This system is used when the public does not directly vote on school tax referenda.

Board of School Trustees: See BOARD OF EDUCATION.

Board Secretary: The person who is responsible for handling the administrative aspects of the board of education, e.g., filing meeting notices, preparing meeting minutes, and organizing information for board decisions. In some cases, this person is also responsible for the district's finances.

Bond Referendum: A question placed before the public on whether or not the school district should issue bonds to pay for one or more projects. Bonds are repaid, with interest, over a period of time, such as 10 or 20 years, out of tax receipts. Once a bond referendum has been approved by the voters, the monies required to repay them are automatically included in the district's tax levy. In other words, money to service the district debt does not appear on the ballot of any subsequent annual budget referendum.

Booster Group: A group whose purpose is to promote an activity, such as an athletic booster club.

Capital Improvement: Construction, purchase, or repair of buildings or equipment.

Capital Outlay: Monies spent to purchase, repair, or improve school buildings or to purchase major items such as school buses.

Central Office: The offices of the board of education and the district administration, including the superintendent of schools.

Charter School: A public school that operates with a special charter from the state, rather than as a traditional school district. The charter may free the school from some of the state regulations binding regular school districts, while holding the school more accountable for student outcomes.

Classroom Aide: See AIDE.

Collaborative Learning: A method of instruction in which students work together in joint intellectual efforts, rather than simply working at a teacher's direction.

Collective Bargaining: The process of negotiating labor contracts.

Compensatory Education: Special remedial assistance provided to students who are not succeeding academically. Critics complain that the practice of removing students from regular classes to provide remediation may penalize them academically and socially.

Competency Test: A test to determine whether a student can perform at a predetermined level in a subject area, such as being able to read, write, or compute as expected for a student at the tenth-grade level.

Consolidation: The practice of merging two or more schools or school districts into a single organizational unit, presumably to achieve financial, administrative, or curricular efficiencies.

Cooperative Learning: See COLLABORATIVE LEARNING.

Criterion-Referenced Test: A test that is scored on how closely a student meets the performance standard set for the test. Some fixed percentage of correct answers is taken to mean that the student has mastered the tasks involved. Compare NORM- REFERENCED TEST.

Current Expenditures: School expenditures for such items as salaries, fixed charges, student transportation, books and materials, and energy costs. Excluded from expenditures are capital outlay and interest on school debt.

Curriculum: The course of study in a particular subject, e.g., the reading curriculum. Sometimes used to refer to all that is meant to be taught in a grade or school, e.g., the fourth-grade curriculum. Plural = curricula.

Curriculum-Based Test: A test, written by teachers or supplied by textbook publishers, which attempts to measure students' grasp of a particular unit of the curriculum studied. Compare STANDARDIZED TEST.

Curriculum Development: The process of creating or modifying courses of study.

Debt Service: Paying back the monies borrowed to make capital improvements.

Desegregation: Eliminating the separation of one group from the main body of society. In education, the practice of ending the practice of educating black and white students in separate schools.

District Administrative Staff: The chief executive officers of school districts, plus all others with district-wide responsibilities, such as business managers, administrative assistants, and coordinators.

District Administrative Support Staff: Personnel assigned to the staffs of district administrators, including clerks, computer programmers, secretaries, and others serving the entire district.

Dropout: A student who ceases to attend a school before graduating, without transferring to another school.

Dropout Rate: A measurement of a school's or school district's ability to encourage its students to remain in attendance through graduation. The rate may be expressed as the percentage of the entire enrollment of grades 9-12 that drops out during a calendar year (including those who fail to return to school after summer vacation) or as the percentage of ninth graders who failed to graduate four years later.

Due Process: A constitutional doctrine that no one can be deprived of life, liberty, or property without proper legal proceedings. Thus, teachers may not be fired, or students expelled, without following a standard process which allows an accused to know and respond to charges against him or her.

Education Foundation: See LOCAL EDUCATION FOUNDATION.

Elementary School: A school composed of any span of grades between kindergarten and grade 8; the grade range is different in some states and localities.

Executive Session: A meeting of a school board (and any other public body) from which the general public is excluded. Such sessions are allowed only under certain circumstances, defined under a state's Open Meetings Act, and usually restricted to discussions on topics — such as personnel issues — deemed too sensitive for public knowledge.

Expenditures: See CURRENT EXPENDITURES.

GED Certificate: A General Education Diploma granted to someone who has not graduated from high school, but who passes a GED test to determine if he or she has equivalent skills and knowledge.

Goals 2000: See AMERICA 2000.

Grouping: Grouping of students in classes (for particular subjects or for all subjects) can be either homogeneous, that is, according to students' assumed abilities, or heterogeneous, that is, without regard to individual abilities.

Guidance Counselor: Professional staff whose duties include counseling students and parents, consulting with other staff members on learning problems, evaluating abilities of students, assisting students in personal and social development, providing referral assistance, and planning and conducting guidance programs.

Handicapped: Children evaluated as having any of the following impairments: deaf; deaf-blind; hard of hearing; mentally retarded; multiply handicapped; orthopedically impaired; other health impaired; seriously emotionally disturbed; specific learning disabled; speech impaired; visually handicapped.

Hands-On Learning: Learning which introduces students to materials or activities related to the topic, in order to give them practical experience in addition to verbal information.

Head Start: A federally-funded pre-school program for children from low-income families, designed to prepare them to take fuller advantage of curriculum in kindergarten and early grades.

Heterogeneous Grouping: See GROUPING.

High School: Any secondary school that includes grades 10-12 (in a 6-3-3 plan) or grades 9-12 (in a 6-2-4 plan).

Home and School Association: Parent/teacher group not affiliated with state and national organizations.

Homogeneous Grouping: See GROUPING.

I Have a Dream Project: A program that attempts to motivate students to complete their secondary schooling by providing them with academic support and committing to pay their college tuition.

Instructional Staff: All public elementary and secondary positions that involve teaching or the improvement of the teaching-learning process, including supervisors of instruction; principals; teachers, guidance personnel; librarians; and psychological personnel. Excludes administrative staff, attendance personnel, and clerical personnel.

IQ Tests: Examinations which purport to measure a student's intelligence; such tests have come under intense criticism in recent decades, because there is no widely accepted definition of intelligence and because any test is likely to contain cultural biases which tend to discriminate against minorities.

Junior High School: A secondary school that is intermediate between elementary and senior high schools; usually includes grades 7-9 (in a 6-3-3 plan) or grades 7-8 (in a 6-2-4 plan).

Local Education Foundation: An independent, non-profit organization established to rally community resources — including money, goods, and volunteer services — to benefit one or more schools or school districts.

Magnet School: A school with a special program that draws students from beyond the normal school boundaries. A magnet school might stress the performing arts, for instance, and draw students from throughout a city or county. Magnet schools are sometimes used to integrate a district's schools.

Mainstreaming: The practice of including students with conditions that hamper learning (such as physical or mental handicaps or insufficient command of English) in educational programs designed for students in general, as opposed to segregating them in special education classes.

Mentor: An adult who is paired with a young person for the purpose of providing guidance and support.

Middle School: A school intermediate between elementary and secondary schools and designed to accommodate needs of students from about age 10 to 14. A typical grade pattern is grades 5-8.

Minimum Basic Skills Test: See MINIMUM-COMPETENCY TEST.

Minimum-Competency Test: A test measuring the acquisition of competence or skills at or beyond a specified minimum standard, often used to determine student eligibility for grade promotion or graduation. See BASIC SKILLS TEST.

Montessori Method: An early childhood education approach which stresses training of the senses and individual guidance. Developed by Italian physician Maria Montessori (1870-1952), the method has become the basis for private schools throughout Europe and the United States. Some American public schools are also organized on Montessori principles.

Multi-Age Grouping: Grouping students into classes regardless of their ages; the result is sometimes called a non-graded school.

Needs Assessment: The process of looking at all facets of a school to determine where improvements are required.

Non-Graded School: See MULTI-AGE GROUPING.

Non-Supervisory Instructional Staff: Staff possessing education certification, but not responsible for day-to-day teaching of the same group of students; includes curriculum specialists, counselors, librarians, and remedial specialists.

Non-Profit Organization: An organization that does not seek a profit and is exempt from tax laws. Non-profits that may be important to schools include foundations, social welfare organizations, public libraries, colleges, and religious groups.

Norm-Referenced Test: A standardized test that measures a student's performance in comparison to that of other students of a specified norm group, such as an age or grade group. Examples include the Stanford Achievement Test, the Comprehensive Test of Basic Skills, and the Scholastic Aptitude Test (SAT). Also see STANDARDIZED TEST and CRITERION-REFERENCED TEST.

Open Meetings Act: State law, sometimes called a "Sunshine" law, requiring public bodies, including school boards, to advertise and hold their meetings in public.

Parent Outreach Program: A program where school staff or parent-teacher group members seek out other parents in the community and attempt to get them involved with schools and their children's learning.

Parent/Teacher Association (PTA): School parent/teacher group affiliated with state and national PTAs.

Parent/Teacher Organization (PTO): School parent/teacher group not affiliated with any state or national groups.

Public Hearing: A meeting where the public is invited to become informed and to air their opinions about a matter.

Pupil/Teacher Ratio: See STUDENT/TEACHER RATIO.

Regional District: A district formed as the result of consolidation of two or more separate school districts, for the purpose of providing educational programs. Several small districts, for example, might create a regional high-school district to provide programs for their students in grades 9-12.

Regular Meeting: A school board meeting at which normal business is conducted; regular meetings are held at a time and place established at the board's annual or reorganization meeting or included in the board's bylaws. Also see EXECUTIVE SESSION.

Remediation: The practice of providing additional help or remedial work in order to correct deficiencies in student skills and knowledge.

Report Card: See SCHOOL REPORT CARD.

Restructuring: The process of reforming schools and school districts so as to fundamentally change the way they operate.

Scholastic Aptitude Test (SAT): A widely used test to determine to what extent high-school students are prepared to handle college-level studies. Average school SAT scores are often and inappropriately used to judge the quality of education delivered. Similarly, average national scores are inappropriately used as a barometer of the quality of public education nation-wide.

School Administrator: Staff member concerned with directing and managing the operation of a particular school, including principals and assistant principals.

School-Based Management: A method of school governance that permits significant decisions about a school to be made by a school-site council. See SCHOOL-SITE COUNCIL.

School Board: See BOARD OF EDUCATION.

School-Business Partnership: A link between one or more schools or school districts and one or more business enterprises, for the purpose of aiding or improving education. This term covers a wide range of activities, from a store that provides jerseys for a high-school basketball team to a consortium of corporations promoting general educational reform throughout the state. An earlier name for some of these activities, "Adopt-A-School" programs, has fallen into general disuse.

School Climate: The social system and culture of a school, including the organizational structure of the school and the values and expectations within it.

School Committee: See BOARD OF EDUCATION.

School Council: See SCHOOL-SITE COUNCIL.

School District: A governmental unit that exists primarily to operate public schools or to contract for public school services. Most school districts in America are organized on a local basis, but some states have county districts, and one — Hawaii — has a single statewide district.

School Foundation: See LOCAL EDUCATION FOUNDATION.

School Improvement Council: See SCHOOL-SITE COUNCIL.

School Report Card: Report on the performance of schools and/or school districts, often issued by the local district; alternatively, some states or statewide organizations issue public reports rating and comparing all schools or school districts in the state.

School-Site Council: A group of people who have some responsibility for making decisions that affect a particular school. These decisions may include hiring and firing of staff (including the principal), allocation of monies provided by the board of education, planning school improvement efforts, and curriculum implementation. In some instances, these councils have real authority; in others, they are advisory in nature. See pages 70-73, 149-150.

School Trustees: School board members.

Site-Based Management: See SCHOOL-BASED MANAGEMENT.

6-3-3 Plan: A school district organizational pattern in which grades 1-6 attend elementary schools, grades 7-9 attend junior high schools, and grades 10-12 attend high schools.

6-2-4 Plan: A school district organizational pattern in which grades 1-6 attend elementary schools, grades 7-8 attend junior high schools, and grades 9-12 attend high schools.

Special Education: School programs designed for children with physical, mental, or emotional handicaps. See HANDICAPPED.

Special Election: An election held for a specific purpose at a time other than a general election, as when a school district elects a board member to fill a mid-term vacancy.

Special Meeting: Any meeting other than a regular or emergency meeting. Such meetings may be called for a particular purpose (a public hearing on a referendum, for instance) or to continue an adjourned session.

Standardized Test: A test, generally developed by publishers or testing companies, which attempts to measure student achievement in comparison to that of a standard group of students who have already taken the test. Compare CURRICULUM-BASED TEST.

Standing Committee: A committee that has an on-going function and no definite end-point.

Student/Staff Ratio: The number of students per professional staff member, including guidance counselors, librarians, and administrators.

Student/Teacher Ratio: The number of students per teacher in a school or school district. The number can be misleading since some teachers — such as special education teachers — have very small classes; thus, a school with a student/teacher ratio of 15:1 might have 20 students in a typical math or English class.

Sunshine Law: See OPEN MEETINGS ACT.

Superintendent of Schools: The chief administrative officer of a school district, generally appointed by the school board.

Suspension: The practice of temporarily dismissing a student from school, in accordance with district disciplinary regulations.

Tax Levy Referendum: A question placed before voters to approve or reject changes in tax levies to support schools.

Teacher Association: An employee organization devoted to issues concerning education and teachers. In states that allow public employees to bargain, the local teacher association is usually the bargaining agent for teachers and, sometimes, for nonprofessional district employees as well. Most local associations are affiliated with either the American Federation of Teachers (AFT) or the National Education Association (NEA).

Teacher License: Certificate granted by state departments of education permitting teachers to practice in a state.

Teacher/Student Ratio: See STUDENT/TEACHER RATIO.

Tenure: Protection from arbitrary dismissal given to teachers and other professional staff after a certain length of time in a position. This practice is defended as protecting employees' freedom of speech and condemned as making it extremely difficult to dismiss ineffective employees.

Tracking: see GROUPING

Tutoring: One-on-one instruction, often provided by volunteers, given to students needing additional help.

Vocational School: A school that provides job training as well as some level of academic study, in order to prepare students for employment in one or more semi-skilled, skilled, or technical occupations.

Volunteer Coordinator: The individual in charge of a volunteer program.

Voucher System: One means of providing school choice, in which students and their parents are given vouchers representing the per-pupil cost of education in a school district. The child may then use that voucher to attend a public school in the district, a public school in another district, or a private school. Proponents of vouchers assert that their use would introduce aspects of the free market into education and that the resulting competition by schools for vouchers would improve schooling. Opponents contend that the practice would increase segregation and further erode the quality of urban public schools.

APPENDICES

A. Names for a Local Education Foundation

B. Sample Mission Statements for a Local Education Foundation

C. Sample Bylaws for a Local Education Foundation

D. Sample Press Release Announcing Formation of a Local Education Foundation

E. Sample Brochure for a New Local Education Foundation

F. Annual Budget for an "I Have A Dream" Project

G. Model Corporate Programs

H. State Departments of Education

APPENDIX A

Names for a Local Education Foundation

Generic Names
Pineville Education Foundation
Pineville Public Education Foundation
Pineville Public Education Fund
Pineville Educational Development Foundation
Fund for Pineville School District
Fund for Pineville Schools

Variations Expressing the Purpose of the Organization
Pineville Foundation
        for Educational Excellence
        for Excellence in Education
        for School Excellence
        for Public School Excellence
        for Quality Education
        for Quality Schools
        for Quality Public Schools

Variations Expressing the Nature of the Organizers
Pineville Citizens for Educational Excellence
        Citizens Foundation for Educational Excellence
        Alliance for Educational Excellence
        Partnership for Educational Excellence
        Council for Educational Excellence
        Business and Citizen Alliance for Educational
            Excellence
        Business and Citizens United for Educational
            Excellence
        Coalition for Educational Excellence

APPENDIX B

Sample Mission Statements for a Local Education Foundation

- The Pineville Education Foundation is an independent, community-based, non-profit organization dedicated to securing private-sector resources and community support for the purpose of enhancing the educational experiences of students in the Pineville School District.

- The Pineville Education Foundation is an independent non-profit organization established to focus private-sector resources on the improvement of educational quality and to strengthen public confidence in and support for the Pineville School District.

- The Pineville Education Foundation is an independent non-profit organization established to help improve the quality of education in the Pineville School District by encouraging efforts to improve the learning environment, increasing the effectiveness of instruction, strengthening student motivation, raising faculty morale, and increasing interaction between the school and the community.

- The Pineville Education Foundation is an independent non-profit organization established to secure resources from individuals, corporations, and foundations, to be distributed to support programs that will stimulate excellence in and mobilize community support for the Pineville School District.

- The Pineville Education Foundation is an independent non-profit organization established to secure resources from individuals, corporations, and foundations, to be distributed to support programs for the benefit of the students in the Pineville School District for which public funding is not available, and which will lead to the overall improvement of the quality of education and an enhancement of community support for public education.

APPENDIX C

Sample Bylaws for a Local Education Foundation

*[Note: Your state may require specific language not
included in these Sample Bylaws. Consult an attorney or
base bylaws on those of existing organizations in your state.]*

ARTICLE I
NAME

The name by which the Corporation shall be known is "The Pineville Education Foundation, Inc."

ARTICLE II
PURPOSE

The purpose of the Foundation shall be:

to encourage, solicit, seek and accept contributions of money and property, real and personal, tangible and intangible, restricted, designated or unrestricted, and to maintain, use and apply the whole or any part thereof (income and principal) to or for the benefit of the Pineville Public School in ways accepted by the Board of Education of the Pineville Public School.

to seek, and assist personnel of the school to seek, grants, endowments and other contributions from individuals, corporations, foundations and local, state and federal governments, their agencies or commissions.

to use appropriate means consistent with the policies of the school to achieve the purposes of the foundation.

to enter into contracts with other persons and corporations under which the Foundation would carry out any and all of the above activities for the Foundation.

to carry on any activity and to deal with and expend any such property or income therefrom for any of the foregoing purposes, without limitation, except such limitations, if any, imposed upon the use of such property, or any portion thereof, by the donor, the Certificate of Incorporation, or any other limitation prescribed by law, provided (a) that no activity shall be such as is not permitted by a corporation exempt from Federal Income Tax under Section 501(c)(3) of the Internal Revenue Code of 1954 or any corresponding provision of the Internal Revenue Code, or as deductible under Section 170(c)(2) of such Code; (b) that the Foundation shall not attempt to influence legislation by propaganda or otherwise, nor shall it intervene in, or participate in, any political campaign on behalf of any candidate for political office; and (c) that no part of the net earnings of the Foundation shall go or inure to the benefit of any member, Director or private individual.

ARTICLE III
MEMBERS

Section 1. Designation of Members. Membership in the Foundation shall be limited to those persons constituting the Board of Directors of the Foundation at any given time.

Section 2. Other Classes of Members. The Directors may establish, change or abolish one or more other classes of members who shall have no voting power in the Corporation, but who may have other privileges of membership on such terms and conditions as the Directors may determine.

ARTICLE IV
BOARD OF DIRECTORS

Section 1. Authority. All corporate powers of the Foundation shall be exercised by or under the authority of the Board of Directors, who shall be the "Trustees" described in [applicable provision of state law]. The Board of Directors shall have the authority:

to elect new members of the Board; to elect a President, one or more Vice Presidents, a Secretary and a Treasurer, all of whom will be elected at the Annual Meeting to serve a term of one year or until a successor is selected.

to contract and pay for services of consultants, lawyers, auditors, appraisers and other such experts as may be required at any time.

to rent space when needed and as may be appropriate for Foundation use.

to decide on appropriate methods to be used to achieve the purposes of the Foundation.

to decide whether or not to accept restricted or designated gifts and to decide under what conditions such gifts shall be accepted, while maintaining consistency with Foundation purposes, objectives and intentions.

to pay all reasonable expenses in connection with securing contributions, grants, endowments, etc.

to maintain a checking account to pay Foundation expenses, the size of which shall be determined by the Board.

when necessary, to set up special checking accounts for fundraising events that require large expense payments and to turn over to the approved depositary the net profits of the events.

Section 2. Number, Term of Office, Election and Qualifications. The number of Directors shall be not less than seven (7) members and not more than fifteen (15) members. Each Director shall serve for a term of three (3) years or until a successor is elected. At the end of the first year, and thereafter, one third of the Directors shall be elected each year at the Annual Meeting by a majority vote of the Directors then in office. Nominations for Director may be submitted by the Nominating Committee or by individual Directors.

Elected Directors shall not include members or employees of the Board of Education of the Pineville Public School District. In addition to the elected Directors, the Superintendent of the Pineville School District and a member of the Board of Education of the Pineville School District, to be chosen by the Board of Education, shall be non-voting Directors of the Foundation by virtue of their office.

Except as otherwise stated in these Bylaws, any vacancy occurring among the members of the Board of Directors shall be filled by a majority vote of the Directors then in office. A Director elected to fill a vacancy shall be elected for the unexpired term of his or her predecessor. By a majority vote of the existing board members, additional directors may be elected, up to the full compliment of directors.

Section 3. Resignation and Removal. Any Foundation Director may resign at any time by written resignation filed with the President of the Foundation. Any Foundation Director may be removed from office with or without cause by the affirmative vote of two-thirds (2/3) of the Foundation Directors.

Section 4. Compensation. No Director shall receive, directly or indirectly, any compensation for his or her services as Director. The Board may authorize reimbursement of reasonable expenses incurred by Board members in connection with attendance at Board meetings and other duties.

Section 5. Meetings. The Annual Meeting of the Board of Directors shall be held in the month of September at such date, time and place as the Board of Directors shall determine. In addition to the Annual Meeting, regular meetings shall be held at least quarterly and shall be called by the President or any two Directors.

Section 6. Notice of Meetings. Notice of the Annual Meeting shall be given to the Directors not more than thirty (30) days nor less than ten (10) days before the meeting. Notice of regular meetings shall be given to all the Directors a minimum of four (4) days prior to the meeting.

The notice requirements contained in these Bylaws may be waived in writing by any Director. All waivers shall be made part of the minutes of the meeting.

Section 7. Quorum. The presence of one-half (1/2) of the entire Board shall be necessary and sufficient to constitute a quorum for the transaction of business at any meeting of the Board. The act of a majority of those present at any meeting, at which there is a quorum, shall be the act of the Foundation, except as may be otherwise specifically provided by statute.

Section 8. Voting. At every meeting, each elected Foundation Director shall be entitled to one vote in person.

Section 9. Action in Lieu of a Meeting. Any Board action required or permitted to be taken by the Board may be taken without a meeting, if two-thirds (2/3) of all members of the Board shall consent in advance to such action in writing. Such written consent shall be made a part of the minutes of the proceedings. Such action by written consent shall have the same force and effect as the same vote of the Directors at a duly convened meeting.

ARTICLE V
OFFICERS

Section 1. Election, Term of Office, Resignation and Removal. The Officers of the Foundation shall be a President, one or more Vice Presidents, a Secretary and a Treasurer, and such other Officers as the Board may from time to time determine.

The Officers shall be elected at the Annual Meeting of the Foundation Board of Directors from among the elected members of the Board of Directors and shall hold office for a one (1) year term or until their successors are elected. All Officers of the Foundation shall hold their respective positions at the pleasure of the Board and may be removed by the Board of Directors with or without cause. Any Officer of the Foundation may resign at any time by written resignation filed with the President of the Foundation. In the event of death, disability, removal or resignation of any Officer of the Foundation, the Board of Directors shall elect a successor to serve out his or her unexpired term.

Section 2. President: Powers and Duties. Subject to the control of the Board of Directors, the President shall have general supervision of the affairs of the Foundation. The President shall preside at all meetings of the Board of Directors and shall have such other duties as may be prescribed by the Board of Directors. The President shall serve as an *ex officio* member of all committees, with the exception of the Nominating Committee.

Section 3. Vice President(s): Powers and Duties. At the request of the President, or in the event of his or her absence or disability, the Vice President (or Vice Presidents in the order of designated seniority) shall perform the duties, and possess and exercise the powers of the President; and to the extent authorized by law, any such Vice President shall have such other powers as the Board of Directors may determine and shall perform such other duties as may be assigned by the Board of Directors.

Section 4. Secretary: Powers and Duties. The Secretary shall have charge of such books, documents and papers as the Board of Directors may determine and shall have custody of the corporate seal. The Secretary shall attend and keep the minutes of all meetings. He or she may, together with the President or any Vice President, sign in the name of or on behalf of the Foundation, any contracts or agreements authorized by the Board of Directors, and when so authorized or ordered by the Board of Directors, may affix the seal of the Foundation. The Secretary shall, in general, perform all the duties incident to the office of Secretary subject to the control of the Board of Directors and shall do and perform such other duties as may be assigned by the Board of Directors.

Section 5. Treasurer: Powers and Duties. The Treasurer shall have the custody of all funds, property and securities of the Foundation, subject to such regulations as may be imposed by the Board of Directors. When necessary or proper, the Treasurer may endorse on behalf of the Foundation for collection checks, notes and other obligations and shall deposit the same to the credit of the Foundation at such bank or banks or depository as the Board of Directors may designate. The Treasurer shall sign all receipts and vouchers, and together with such other Officer or Officers, if any, as shall be designated by the Board of Directors, shall sign all checks of the Foundation, except in cases where the signing and execution thereof shall be expressly designated by the Board of Directors or by these Bylaws to some other Officer or agent of the Foundation. The Treasurer shall make such payments as may be necessary or proper to be made on behalf of the Foundation and shall enter regularly on the books of the Foundation, to be kept by him or her for that purpose, full and accurate account of all moneys and obligations received and paid or incurred by him or her for or on account of the Foundation, and shall exhibit such books at all reasonable times to any Foundation Director on application of the Officers of the Foundation. The Treasurer shall submit an annual report at the Annual Meeting, as well as such other reports as may be required by the Board of Directors from time to time. He or she shall, in general, perform all the duties incident to the office of Treasurer, subject to the control of the Board of Directors.

ARTICLE VI
COMMITTEES

Section 1. Appointment. Except as otherwise stated in these Bylaws, the President shall appoint the members and designate the chair of standing and other committees. Committees shall serve at the pleasure of the Board under such rules and regulations as the Board may approve.

Section 2. Standing Committees. There shall be a Finance Committee, the responsibilities of which shall include fact-finding for the Board on matters relating to the financial administration of the Foundation and preparation of the annual budget for presentation to the Board. The Treasurer shall serve on the committee *ex officio*.

There shall be a Program Committee, the responsibilities of which shall include recommending to the Board of Directors what programs the Foundation should undertake on behalf of the Pineville School District.

There shall be a Fundraising Committee, the responsibilities of which shall include planning for the solicitation of contributions in support of the Foundation's purposes.

There shall be a Nominating Committee of not less than three (3) persons, which shall present nominations for Directors and Officers.

There shall be a Public Information Committee, the responsibilities of which shall include planning a program to promote understanding and acceptance of the Foundation by the community.

Section 3. Other Committees. The Board of Directors may create additional board committees and citizen advisory committees, as needed.

ARTICLE VII
FINANCES

Funds of the Foundation shall be deposited in a bank under national or state supervision. The Board of Directors shall authorize an appropriate individual or individuals to sign negotiable instruments on behalf of the Foundation.

There shall be an annual audit by an independent accounting firm within ninety (90) days of the close of the fiscal year.

ARTICLE VIII
INDEMNIFICATION

Each Foundation Director and Officer, whether or not then in office, and his or her heirs, executors, administrators and assigns, shall be indemnified by the Foundation against all costs and expenses reasonably incurred by or imposed upon him or her, or his or her estate, in connection with or resulting from any action, suit or proceeding, civil or criminal, to which he or she, or his or her estate, shall or may be a party, or with which he or she or it shall or may be threatened by reason, directly or indirectly, of his or her being or having been a Director or Officer of the Foundation, except in relation to matters as to which he or she shall be finally adjudged in such action, suit or proceeding to be liable for malfeasance or gross negligence in the performance of his or her duty as such Director or Officer. Each Foundation Director and Officer shall also be indemnified against any costs or expenses reasonably incurred by or imposed upon him or her, or his or her estate, in connection with or resulting from the settlement of any such action, suit or proceeding in which such Director or Officer was not liable for malfeasance or gross negligence in the performance of his or her duty as Director or Officer. The costs and expenses against which any such Director or Officer shall be indemnified shall be those actually paid or for which liability is actually incurred, irrespective of whether such costs or expenses are taxable costs as defined or allowed by statute or rule of court. A Director or Officer shall not be deemed to have been liable for malfeasance or gross negligence in the performance of his or her duty as a Director or Officer as to any matter wherein he or she relied upon the opinion or advice of legal counsel selected by the Board of Directors or acting in any such matter for the Foundation. Such rights of indemnification shall be in addition to any other right with respect to any such costs and expenses to which such Director or Officer may otherwise be entitled against the Foundation or any other persons.

ARTICLE IX
DISSOLUTION

Upon the dissolution or other termination of the Foundation, no part of the property of the Foundation or any of the proceeds shall be distributed to or inure to the benefit of any of the Directors or Officers of the Foundation, but all such property and proceeds, subject to the discharge of valid obligations of the Foundation, shall be distributed exclusively to Federal, State or Local government bodies or to other charitable or educational organizations which then qualify under the provisions of Section 501(c)(3) of the Internal Revenue Code and the Regulations as they now exist or as they may hereafter be amended.

ARTICLE X
MISCELLANEOUS PROVISIONS

Section 1. Fiscal Year. The Fiscal Year of the Foundation shall begin on July 1 of each year.

Section 2. Rules of Parliamentary Procedure. Robert's Rules of Order, in its most recent edition at the date of its use, shall be the parliamentary authority for all matters of procedure not specifically covered by these Bylaws or by other specific rules of procedure adopted by the Directors of the Foundation.

ARTICLE XI
AMENDMENT OF BYLAWS

The Bylaws of the Foundation may be amended by two-thirds (2/3) vote of all the Foundation Directors at an annual or regular meeting of the Board, provided notice of the character of the proposed amendment shall have been given to the Directors at least twenty (20) days before such amendment is voted upon. Such amendments shall be consistent with the purpose, objectives and intentions of the Foundation. The Secretary of the Foundation shall at all times keep in the office of the Foundation a true and correct copy of the Bylaws.

Sample Press Release Announcing Formation of a Local Education Foundation

December 1, 1994
FOR IMMEDIATE RELEASE

For further information
contact: Wyatt Gwyon
at (123) 456-7890

Foundation Formed to Benefit Pineville Public Schools

A group of Pineville citizens and business people today announced formation of a new foundation dedicated to the support of the Pineville Public Schools. Victor Johnson, president of Pineville Hospital, was named chairman of the group's board of directors.

The new organization, the Pineville Education Foundation (PEF), will be a non-profit corporation which its founders hope will attract tax-deductible contributions and volunteer assistance to the Pineville Public Schools from a variety of sources. While it will be completely independent of the school district and the board of education, the foundation will seek the school board's approval of any programs it wishes to initiate and any donations it wishes to make.

The foundation arose from meetings of a steering committee, convened by Pineville National Bank President John J. French to study ways of providing community support to the school district. The committee, composed of people who either live or conduct business in Pineville, became the board of directors of the new foundation when the decision was made to incorporate.

Besides Johnson and French, the members of the board are Hugo Barish, of Hammond and Barish; Cliff Cardell, of Barney Associates; James Conroy, Vice President for Community Affairs at Chemical Corporation of America; Susan Rose, Director of the Pineville YMCA; John J. Gunther, an attorney with Burney and Burney;

Stephen F. Hebble, Director of External Affairs for the United Electric and Gas Company; and David M. Brody, of White Mountain Realty Company.

All will serve on the foundation board of directors, with French as vice-chair, Rose as treasurer, and Hebble as secretary. Superintendent of Schools Arthur Field will sit on the board as a nonvoting member.

There are hundreds of successful local education foundations throughout the United States, some of which have been credited with raising substantial sums and increasing public support for the public schools. About ten active organizations exist in this state. Typically, such foundations solicit money, goods, and services from foundations, corporations, and community members, and dedicate them to school programs chosen by the local foundation and approved by the board of education.

In his announcement of the PEF's formation, Johnson emphasized the community nature of the foundation and expressed the hope that it would become the catalyst for increased citizen involvement in and support for the schools. "We're looking for support from people who realize that the future of our community is dependent on the quality of our public education system," Johnson said. "We hope to attract contributions from businesses and ordinary citizens which we can offer as seed money for exciting new programs in the schools. We'll never replace tax dollars as the basic support for education, but we think we can inspire donations of money and equipment which can bring far-reaching innovations to the classroom."

Johnson encouraged interested citizens to contact him by calling (123) 456-7890 or writing to Pineville Education Foundation, 65 Chestnut Street, Pineville.

Sample Brochure for a New Local Education Foundation

What is the Pineville Education Foundation?

It's a new citizens organization dedicated to supporting the Pineville Public Schools. Our mission is to mobilize community support, concern, commitment, and resources to help improve the quality of education in Pineville.

Why does Pineville need this kind of help?

Public schools all over America need this kind of help! It's not enough just to pay our school taxes or to support schools only while our kids are in them. America is falling behind in international competition partly because our educational system is not keeping up with the demands of the contemporary world. We believe that if we are to maintain and improve our way of life and our standard of living, millions of Americans must play a more active part in making our educational system the best in the world. We can't change the whole country, but we think we can make a difference here in our own community.

Do foundations like this exist elsewhere?

Yes, there are thousands of education foundations all over the United States. Many foundations have established impressive track records in terms of the support they have generated for local schools.

Is the Pineville Foundation run by the school board?

No, the Foundation is completely independent of the school board and school administration, though we hope to have a cooperative relationship with both. We will need to know about their priorities and needs. And the law requires the board to approve any donations or other assistance we wish to offer.

What kind of support will the Foundation offer to the Pineville Public Schools?

It's hard to be specific when we are just getting started. The Foundation is going to look for new ideas which can have real benefits for students, but which are not likely to be funded by taxes. It could be mini-grants for innovative classroom activities; or solicitation of used computers or equipment; or a program to bring local artists into the school; or a campaign to recruit volunteers to tutor students having difficulties in their classes. The

Foundation will seek donations of funds, goods, and services to make the ideas a reality. In some cases, the school board may vote to fund continuation of a project we have inspired; if so, we'll look for new areas where we can help.

Is it possible that the Foundation will lower our school taxes?

No. We'll never raise that much money and it's not our purpose. We just want to provide small sums at critical times and apply them to key programs as a catalyst for school improvement. We hope that such funds — and the goods and volunteers we recruit — can help the district spark innovation and excellence. Your taxes will go on supporting the bulk of school programs.

Who is involved in this Foundation?

Local citizens who are convinced that the success of the school district is linked to the well-being of the entire community. The current board of directors consists of:

> Victor Johnson, President, Pineville Hospital — Chair
> John J. French, President, Pineville National Bank —
>   Vice-Chair
> Susan Rose, Director, Pineville YMCA — Treasurer
> Stephen F. Hebble, Director of External Affairs, United Electric and
>   Gas Company — Secretary
> Hugo Barish, Hammond and Barish
> David M. Brody, White Mountain Realty Company
> Cliff Cardell, Barney Associates
> James Conroy, Vice President for Community Affairs, Chemical
>   Corporation of America
> John J. Gunther, Esq., Burney and Burney

The Foundation sounds like a great idea! How can I help?

We need four kinds of help:
> (1) you can help us inform the community about who we are and
>   what we hope to accomplish;
> (2) you can contribute your expertise (we need occasional help with
>   legal advice, accounting, public relations, printing, etc.);
> (3) you can volunteer to help us campaign for funds or equipment to
>   benefit the students of the district; and
> (4) you can make tax-deductible contributions to help us achieve our
>   mission.

To offer assistance or to find out more about us, speak to any member of our board or call Victor Johnson, President, Pineville Education Foundation, at 123-4567.

APPENDIX F

Annual Budget for an "I Have a Dream" Project

Personnel:

Project Coordinator	$32,000	
Employee Benefits @ 20%	6,400	
Subtotal		$38,400

Other Expenses:

Transportation	1,000	
Food, Favors, Parties, Trips	2,000	
Photocopy & Printing	500	
Postage	400	
Office Supplies	300	
Telephone	500	
IHAD Convention Participation	1,000	
Temporary Help	500	
National IHAD Foundation Dues	2,000	
Miscellaneous	2,400	
Subtotal		10,600
Local IHAD Fdn./CBO Overhead Subtotal		7,350
@ 15% (includes items such as secretarial services, office space costs, insurance, other activities for young people, supervision)		
TOTAL		$56,350

This is the estimated minimum annual cost of operating an IHAD Project involving 40-75 Dreamers. It could be operated within a plus-or-minus 15% range. The present value of the above budget, allowing for a conservative 4% annual increase of its total for ten years (assuming a third-grade Project start) would be $367,400. Assuming a 10% budget reduction, the present value would be $330,000. IHAD Fdn. = I Have a Dream Foundation; CBO = Community Based Organization. One of these would administer the Project.

APPENDIX G

Model Corporate Programs

Agents of Change, a 1993 booklet published by the Education Task Force of The Business Roundtable, provides copious examples of successful corporate initiatives on behalf of public schools and valuable advice on how to structure involvement. Included are programs encouraging and supporting employee volunteer efforts as well as projects in which employees may get involved in a variety of roles. The following excerpts, while concentrating on activities of major corporations, may provide inspiration and encouragement to executives and employees at companies of all sizes.

- For all its employee volunteers who will work in classrooms, Eastman Kodak provides not only training in teaching techniques but a special orientation program that covers school culture and environment, the stages of a child's development, and cultural diversity.

- Several corporations with major operations in Chicago — among them Amoco, AT&T, Illinois Bell, and CNA Insurance — have encouraged employees to run for local school councils. The companies provide training for employees who seek election, and follow-up support for those elected who are serving on these councils. The Amoco Educators Club, for one, supports its council members — and other employees on suburban school boards — through help with public and media relations, legal advice, writing and editing services, referral services, and further training. Monthly club meetings give employees a chance to discuss successes and frustrations. CNA Insurance provides comparable support.

- Chrysler Corp. runs forums for prospective school board members, with sessions on board member responsibilities and how to run an effective campaign.

- IBM launched a "school volunteer hotline" in the San Francisco Bay Area. Using a computer database, it provides information about local volunteer opportunities in K-12 schools for IBM employees and other citizens.

- Chevron Corporation's computerized VOICE ("Volunteer Opportunities Involving Chevron Employees") program invites requests for volunteers from schools and local non-profit organizations, and disseminates them among employees via electronic mail. Chevron also set out to mobilize interest in business involvement in education in the San Francisco Bay Area through underwriting a year-long series of monthly articles in the

San Francisco Business Times. The Times also published a guide to national, state, and local organizations involved in programs aimed at strengthening education.

● Unum, in Maine, has a Volunteer Data Bank to match employee volunteers with schools engaged in restructuring.

● Some corporations offer incentives to promote employee volunteerism. Aetna Life & Casualty is credited with originating the "Dollars for Doers" program, in which its foundation provides special-need grants up to $500 to schools and other nonprofit organizations where Aetna employees volunteer.

● In its "Dollars for Doers" program, the Scott Paper Company Foundation contributes up to $250 to schools or other eligible nonprofit organizations where a Scott employee, retiree, or director has volunteered for 40 hours in a six-month period, or up to $500 for 80 hours or more in a calendar year.

● McGraw-Hill's foundation provides grants up to $1,000 to PTAs, cultural and literacy groups, and other organizations in which employees have substantial ongoing involvement. Employees must be volunteering with the organizations at least 30 hours a year, and must have been involved for more than one year.

● When Chevron decided to support the Accelerated Schools Program devised by Stanford University Prof. Henry M. Levin, it picked four satellite sites in cities where it had substantial numbers of employees who could later be recruited as volunteers.

● McDonnell Douglas, in St. Louis, began the Homework Hotline nine years ago. In the fall of 1991, the company merged its program with the Missouri National Education Association (MNEA)'s Homework Hotline run by retired teachers. The volunteers don't give out answers, but instead help guide students to discover the answers for themselves and master skills necessary to understand the problem-solving process. In the partnership's first year, the volunteers received some 30,000 calls — averaging 150 to 250 per night.

● New England Electric System, after establishing a "family" of 13 Partnership Schools in three states, now publishes a newsletter, *The Partnership Line,* to link the partnerships and provide news articles and photos of their activities,

● Federal Express has been paired for more than a decade with Booker T. Washington High School in inner-city Memphis under an adopt-a-school program. Major features of this relationship have been "development clubs" led by Federal Express employees in subjects ranging from finance, engineering, and customer service to creative arts, secretarial science, and social responsibility. Employees serve as role models, inform and motivate them, initiate projects, take them on tours, conduct career fairs, sponsor contests, and recognize achievements.

- GenCorp, in Akron Ohio, has developed a program for 6th graders at an inner-city middle school designed to show them the relevancy between school and work, motivate them to finish school and prepare for the job market, boost self-esteem and work-ethic attitudes, learn teamwork, and increase reading skills. The program involves placing class members into three "companies," in which each has a job, and puts them to work under guidance of company advisers and teachers. Students are paid in "BEAR Bucks" that they can spend to buy products from a catalog. Rebecca Gilliam, GenCorp director of equal opportunity and affirmative action, is writing a "how to" manual so the project can be replicated.

- Kroger developed a program in an inner-city Cincinnati elementary school in which it installed a miniature supermarket in a vacant classroom. Students "shop" with points (worth up to $9 a week) earned for attendance, good behavior and academic improvement. While Kroger volunteers supervise, the older students stock shelves, price products, run cash registers, and provide security.

- In East Hartford, United Technologies' Pratt & Whitney Division enlisted 18 volunteers from its engineering department to serve as profession advisors to 22 advanced math and science students at East Hartford High School. The corporation brought high school teachers with the students to visit its facilities so they could learn about job skills related to their subjects and thus be able to teach more realistically and effectively.

- In Tenneco's partnership with Jefferson Davis High School near downtown Houston dating back to 1981, employee mentoring and tutoring has long been a mainstay. In 1989, the company went further — helping create an education collaborative in which the University of Houston-Downtown, the Metropolitan Organization (a coalition of 60 local churches), and Communities in Schools (a social-services program) are now also involved in joint efforts to help more students to graduate from Davis and attend college. The centerpiece is Tenneco's Presidential Scholarship program, which guarantees $1,000-a-year college scholarships to students who maintain satisfactory grades in core courses, take three years of math, and complete two summer sessions (or the equivalent) at university-based institutes.

- Kmart Corporation is also collaborating with a university — to help a projected 300 juniors and seniors at several inner-city St. Louis high schools. In the KEY (Kmart Employment for Youth) Work Force 2000 program, Kmart and the University of Missouri-St. Louis provide employment readiness training, work opportunities in Kmart stores, and — for outstanding participants — scholarships to the university for up to $1,000 a year.

- In Cincinnati, Proctor & Gamble President John E. Pepper is co-chair of the Cincinnati Youth Collaborative, which has launched a variety of education projects involving hundreds of mentors, tutors, and other volunteers. P&G has also been actively involved since 1987 in Project Aspire, a partnership with Woodward High School and its mostly minority students. Project Aspire began as a mentoring project and has expanded to include career counseling, tutoring, and other services.

- Project management concerns infuse a 10-year "model school reform partnership," which Union Carbide, its foundation, and the St. Charles, Louisiana school system signed in October 1991. The school system agreed to build community support for the project's "vision" (based on The Business Roundtable's nine components for success). It also agreed to develop: performance-based outcomes and means to assess them for the system and individual schools; site-based management for individual schools; a system of rewards and "corrective actions" for individual schools based on their outcomes performance; and a system of fiscal accountability. Union Carbide will help the school system muster community support for change; provide staff for developing strategy, and counseling and support for communicating goals, needs, methods, and procedures; and support the school system's strategic plan by disseminating statements to its employees and the community. The foundation will commit up to $150,000 a year over 10 years.

- TRW has played key roles in launching the California Academy of Mathematics and Sciences (CAMS), a specialized high school on the campus of California State University, Dominguez Hills. The TRW Foundation leads an extensive list of companies and foundations that support CAMS with cash and equipment contributions. Industry sources provide about 30 percent of the innovative school's total operating budget. TRW employees also serve as mentors, teachers, speakers, tutors, and technical advisers.

- Continental Bank in Chicago and Orr Community Academy High School initiated a partnership in 1989 called the Orr School Network, involving the bank, Orr, and its 12 "feeder" elementary schools. The project's goal is to apply a community approach to school improvement, connecting the schools with each other and with the educational, cultural, and social-service resources of the city. Bank employees volunteer as mentors and academic "coaches."

- In Philadelphia, CIGNA developed a Neighborhood School Partnership with five schools in a South Philadelphia neighborhood that represent a "feeder" system from pre-kindergarten through high school. In CIGNA's related "Learning, Friends and Fun" project, 90 CIGNA employees were tutoring second, third, and fourth graders one hour a week on CIGNA premises.

- IBM has 12 partnerships with schools in California's Santa Clara County. It commits senior managers to work with senior school administrators for each school partnership. IBM assigns employees to teach particular classes, judge science fairs, and engage in other activities. More ambitious has been IBM's collaboration with the Austin, Texas School District in mounting "Project A+." Early accomplishments included introducing the "MegaSkills" program in 38 of Austin's 65 elementary schools, establishing technology demonstration programs at four elementary schools, and establishing school-based "improvement" programs at another 16 schools.

- The General Electric Foundation's College Bound program targets high school students, with a goal of doubling the number of college-bound students from selected low-income and inner-city schools and assuring their success once in college. General Electric relies on volunteers from its Elfun Society, a community service organization comprising 33,000 middle and upper-middle managers. Elfun chapters have developed school partnerships in recent years in more than 40 cities. For College Bound, the GE Foundation invites selected school districts, which have schools with poor college-going rates but turnaround potential, to submit proposals for grants. The grants pay for training, enrichment, and curriculum development opportunities for teachers; SAT prep classes; college visits; "after-school academies;" parent programs; scholarships; cultural activities, and the like. Students and parents sign "contracts" agreeing to meet school attendance and achievement criteria.

- LEARN (Los Angeles Educational Alliance for Restructuring Now) is a privately financed coalition of civic leaders and other representatives of that diverse city's business, labor, academic, educational, religious, and social advocacy constituencies. Its goal is to build an agenda for the reform and restructuring of Los Angeles schools and then mobilize the community behind implementing this agenda at all levels of government. Key agenda proposals cover school-based management and accountability; greater parent involvement; training for teachers, principals, and others involved in education; strengthening the curriculum; effective involvement of health and social services; improving school facilities and environments, and fiscal restructuring. LEARN publishes *Learning Curve*, a newsletter, and also produces generic speeches, news releases, and "Tell-a-Friend" letters for use by community leaders and groups.

- Amoco scientists played key roles a few years ago in helping the Tulsa, Oklahoma school system enrich its elementary-school science curriculum and boost the test scores of fourth and fifth graders. The scientists developed the new curriculum, acquired equipment for lab experiments, and trained teachers and community volunteers.

- Capital Holding Corp., in Louisville, Kentucky, has worked with the Jefferson County school system to develop a year-long, 11th grade elective in which students learn computing, problem-solving, and decision-making skills plus knowledge of economics, real-world business operations, and the American work ethic.

- General Motors has developed "Explore the Possibilities," a program to encourage junior high school students, especially minorities and young women, to study more math and science and consider careers in engineering and skilled trades. The program relates what students learn in math and science with what engineers and skilled tradespeople apply in their work. GM has developed a handy "implementation manual" and believes that "Explore the Possibilities" has great potential as a model for corporations in other industries to use for launching programs of their own.

- **Employee Loan Programs:** IBM loaned 17 professionals over a three-year period to participate in the MESA (Mathematics Engineering Science Achievement) program in California, which helps promising minority students enter and successfully complete college preparatory programs and go on to attain college degrees; a Hewlett-Packard employee on full-time "loan" has directed the East Side Academies program in San Jose, California, which targets potential dropouts and encourages them to enter a special high school electronics program; Chevron loaned an executive for four months to the Contra Costa County education office to help develop a school volunteer program; Xerox has loaned one executive to serve as corporate secretary of the New American Schools Development Corp., and two executives with particular skills in TQM (Total Quality Management) and human resources to the Center for Education and the Economy in Rochester, NY.

State Departments of Education

Alabama
Superintendent of Education
State Department of Education
Gordon Persons Office Building
50 North Ripley Street
Montgomery, AL 36130-3901
(205) 242-9700

Alaska
Commissioner of Education
State Department of Education
Alaska State Office Building, Pouch F
Juneau, AK 99811
(907) 465-2800

Arizona
Superintendent of Public Instruction
State Department of Education
1535 West Jefferson Street
Phoenix, AZ 85007
(602) 542-4361

Arkansas
Director, General Education Division
State Department of Education
Four State Capitol Mall, Room 304A
Little Rock, AR 72201-1071
(501) 682-4204

California
Superintendent of Public Instruction
State Department of Education
721 Capitol Mall
Sacramento, CA 95814
(916) 657-5485

Colorado
Commissioner of Education
State Department of Education
201 East Colfax Ave.
Denver, CO 80203-1705
(303) 866-6806

Connecticut
Commissioner of Education
State Department of Education
165 Capitol Ave., Room 305
Hartford, CT 06106
(203) 566-5061

Delaware
Superintendent of Public Instruction
State Department of Public Instruction
P.O. Box 1402
Dover, DE 19903
(302) 739-4601

District of Columbia
Superintendent of Public Schools
District of Columbia Public Schools
415 12th Street, NW
Washington, DC 20004
(202) 724-4222

Florida
Commissioner of Education
State Department of Education
Capitol Building, Room PL 08
Tallahassee, FL 32301
(904) 487-1785

Georgia
Superintendent of Schools
State Department of Education
2066 Twin Towers East
Atlanta, GA 30334
(404) 656-2800

Hawaii
Superintendent of Education
Department of Education
1390 Miller Street, # 307
Honolulu, HI 96804
(808) 586-3230

Idaho
Superintendent of Public Instruction
State Department of Education
650 West State Street
Boise, ID 83720
(208) 334-3300

Illinois
Superintendent of Education
State Department of Education
100 North First Street
Springfield, IL 62777
(217) 782-2221

Indiana
Superintendent of Public Instruction
State Department of Education
State House, Room 229
Indianapolis, IN 46204-2798
(317) 232-6665

Iowa
Director of Education
State Department of Education
Grimes State Office Building
East 14th and Grand Streets
Des Moines, IA 50319-0146
(515) 281-5294

Kansas
Commissioner of Education
State Department of Education
120 South East 10th Street
Topeka, KS 66612
(913) 296-3202

Kentucky
Commissioner of Education
State Department of Education
Capitol Plaza Tower
500 Metro Street
Frankfort, KY 40601
(502) 564-3141

Louisiana
Superintendent of Education
State Department of Education
P.O. Box 94064
Baton Rouge, LA 70804-9064
(504) 342-3602

Maine
Commissioner of Education
Maine Department of Education
State House Station 23
Augusta, ME 04333
(207) 287-5114

Maryland
Superintendent of Schools
State Department of Education
200 West Baltimore Street
Baltimore, MD 21201
(410) 333-2200

Massachusetts
Commissioner of Education
State Department of Education
Quincy Center Plaza
1385 Hancock Street
Quincy, MA 02169
(617) 770-7321

Michigan
Superintendent of Public Instruction
State Department of Education
P.O. Box 30008
Lansing, MI 48909
(517) 373-3354

Minnesota
Commissioner of Education
State Department of Education
712 Capitol Square Building
550 Cedar Street
St. Paul, MN 55101
(612) 296-2358

Mississippi
Superintendent of Education
State Department of Education
P.O. 771
Jackson, MS 39205-0771
(601) 359-3513

Missouri
Commissioner of Education
Department of Elementary and
  Secondary Education
P.O. Box 480
Jefferson City, MO 65102
(314) 751-4446

Montana
Superintendent of Public Instruction
State Office of Public Instruction
106 State Capitol
Helena, MT 59620
(406) 444-3680

Nebraska
Commissioner of Education
State Department of Education
P.O. Box 94987
South Lincoln, NE 68509
(402) 471-5020

Nevada
Superintendent of Public Instruction
State Department of Education
400 West King Street
Carson City, NV 89710
(702) 687-3100

New Hampshire
Commissioner of Education
State Department of Education
State Office Park
101 Pleasant Street
South Concord, NH 03301
(603) 271-3144

New Jersey
Commissioner of Education
State Department of Education
CN 500
Trenton, NJ 08625-0500
(609) 292-4450

New Mexico
Superintendent of Public Instruction
State Department of Education Building
300 Don Gaspar
Santa Fe, NM 87501-2786
(505) 827-6516

New York
Commissioner of Education
State Education Department
111 Education Building
Washington Avenue
Albany, NY 12234
(518) 474-5844

North Carolina
Superintendent of Public Instruction
State Department of Public Instruction
Education Building, Room 194
116 West Edenton Street
Raleigh, NC 27603-1712
(919) 733-3813

North Dakota
Superintendent of Public Instruction
State Department of Public Instruction
State Capitol Building, 11th Floor
600 Boulevard Avenue
East Bismarck, ND 58505-0440
(701) 224-2261

Ohio
Superintendent of Public Instruction
State Department of Education
65 South Front Street, Room 808
Columbus, OH 43266-0308
(614) 466-3304

Oklahoma
Superintendent of Public Instruction
State Department of Education
Oliver Hodge Memorial Education Building
2500 North Lincoln Blvd.
Oklahoma City, OK 73105-4599
(405) 521-3301

Oregon
Superintendent of Public Instruction
State Department of Education
700 Pringle Parkway, SE
Salem, OR 97310
(503) 378-3573

Pennsylvania
Secretary of Education
State Department of Education
333 Market Street, 10th Floor
Harrisburg, PA 17126-0333
(717) 787-5820

Rhode Island
Commissioner of Education
State Department of Education
22 Hayes Street
Providence, RI 02908
(401) 277-2031

South Carolina
Superintendent of Education
State Department of Education
1006 Rutledge Building
1429 Senate Street
Columbia, SC 29201
(803) 734-8492

South Dakota
Secretary of Education
Dept of Education and Cultural Affairs
700 Governors Drive
Pierre, SD 57501
(605) 773-3134

Tennessee
Commissioner of Education
State Department of Education
100 Cordell Hull Building
Nashville, TN 37219
(615) 741-2731

Texas
Commissioner of Education
Texas Education Agency
1701 North Congress Avenue
Austin, TX 78701-1494
(512) 463-8985

Utah
Superintendent of Public Instruction
State Office of Education
250 East 500 South
Salt Lake City, UT 84111
(801) 538-7510

Vermont
Commissioner of Education
State Department of Education
120 State Street
Montpelier, VT 05602-2703
(802) 828-3135

Virginia
Superintendent of Public Instruction
State Department of Education
James Monroe Building
14th and Franklin Streets
Richmond, VA 23216-2060
(804) 225-2023

Washington
Superintendent of Public Instruction
State Department of Public Instruction
P.O. Box 47200
Olympia, WA 98504
(206) 586-6904

West Virginia
Superintendent of Schools
State Department of Education
1900 Kanawha Blvd.
East Building 6, Room B-358
Charleston, WV 25305
(304) 558-2681

Wisconsin
Superintendent of Public Instruction
State Department of Public Instruction
P.O. Box 7841
Madison, WI 53707
(608) 266-1771

Wyoming
Superintendent of Public Instruction
State Department of Education
2300 Capitol Avenue, 2nd Floor
Hathaway Building
Cheyenne, WY 82002-0050
(302) 777-7675

Endnotes

1. Wallace Terry, "Make Things Better For Somebody," *Parade Magazine*, February 14, 1993.

2. Harold Hodgkinson, "Reform Versus Reality," *Phi Delta Kappan*, September 1991, p. 10.

3. Diane Ravitch and Chester E. Finn, Jr., *What Do Our 17-Year-Olds Know?* (New York: Harper & Row, 1987), p. 1.

4. Archie E. Lapointe, Nancy A. Mead, and Janice M. Askew, *Learning Mathematics* and *Learning Science* (Princeton, NJ: Educational Testing Service, Reports No. 22-CAEP-01 and No. 22-CAEP-02, 1992).

5. *Being a School Partner: A Guide for Older Volunteers* (Washington, D.C.: American Association of Retired Persons, 1989).

6. As reported in *School Board Notes*, December 10, 1992 (Trenton, NJ: The New Jersey School Boards Association).

7. Stanley M. Elam, Lowell C. Rose, and Alec M. Gallup, "The 24th Annual Gallup/Phi Delta Kappa Poll of the Public's Attitudes Toward the Public Schools," *Phi Delta Kappan*, September 1992, pp. 41-53.

8. Jonathan Kozol, *Savage Inequalities: Children in America's Schools* (New York: Crown Publishers, 1991).

9. Thomas B. Corcoran, Lisa J. Walker, and J. Lynne White, *Working in Urban Schools* (Washington, D.C.: Institute for Educational Leadership, 1988).

10. Michael Meyer, "Another Lost Generations: California schools are overflowing — and broke," *Newsweek*, May 4, 1992, p. 71.

11. Anne C. Lewis, "An Invisible Minority," *Phi Delta Kappan*, May 1992, pp. 660-661.

12. Susan Chira, "Quality Time for Quality Schools," *New York Times*, March 30, 1992.

13. U.S. Department of Education, *What Works: Schools That Work, Educating Disadvantaged Children* (U.S. Government Printing Office, 1987).

14. Michael Ryan, "They Don't Want Thanks," *Parade Magazine*, December 20, 1992, p. 22.

15. Cynthia Parsons, "SerVermont: The Little Initiative That Could," *Phi Delta Kappan*, June, 1991, pp. 768-770; Larry Martz, *Making Schools Better: How Parents and Teachers Across the Country Are Taking Action — And How You Can, Too* (New York: Times Books, 1992).

16. *Chronicle of Philanthropy*, June 30, 1992.

17. *The Nation's Great Unrecognized Resource: The Contributions of Americans 55+* (New York: Commonwealth Fund, n.d.).

18. *New York Times*, December 27, 1992, Business Section.

19. Steven Waldman and Karen Springen, "Too Old, Too Fast?" *Newsweek*, November 16, 1992, p. 80.

20. Susan Chira, "Quality Time for Quality Schools: In Budget Crunch, New York Parents Aid Public Education," *New York Times*, March 30, 1992.

21. Adapted from Barbara J. Hansen, *School Improvement Councils: A Guide to Effectiveness* (Columbia, SC: School Council Assistance Project, College of Education, University of South Carolina, 1989).

22. Barbara J. Hansen and Carl L. Marburger, *School Based Improvement: A Manual for Training School Councils* (Washington, DC: National Committee for Citizens in Education, 1989).

23. Gerald Grant, et al., *On Competence: A Critical Analysis of Competence-Based Reforms in Higher Education* (San Francisco: Jossey-Bass, 1979).

24. C. Reid Rundell, "NASDC: A Businessman's Experience," *Phi Delta Kappan*, December 1992, pp. 290-295.

25. "Citing Other Obstacles, Head of NASDC Resigns," *Education Week*, March 3, 1993, p. 5.

26. James A. Mecklenburger, "The Braking of the 'Break-the-Mold' Express," *Phi Delta Kappan*, December 1992, pp. 280-289.

27. *Met-Life Teachers' Survey, 1992* (New York: Metropolitan Life Insurance Co., 1992).

28. Stanley M. Elam, Lowell C. Rose, and Alec M. Gallup, "The 23rd Annual Gallup Poll of the Public's Attitudes Toward the Public Schools," *Phi Delta Kappan*, September 1991, pp. 41-56, and "The 24th Annual Gallup/Phi Delta Kappa Poll," *Phi Delta Kappan*, September 1992, pp. 41-53.

29. Helen Pate-Bain, et al., "Class Size Does Make a Difference," *Phi Delta Kappan*, November 1992, pp. 253-256.

30. *Newsweek*, October 26, 1992, p. 58.

31. Adapted from Barbara J. Hansen, *School Improvement Councils: A Guide to Effectiveness* (Columbia, SC: The School Council Assistance Project, College of Education, University of So. Carolina, 1989).

INDEX